UNLOCKING GENRE
FOR EAL STUDENTS

Building Transferable Language Skills through Modelled Texts

BONEY NATHAN

Published in 2024 by Amba Press, Melbourne, Australia
www.ambapress.com.au

© Boney Nathan 2024

All rights reserved. No part of this book may be reproduced or transmitted in any form or by any means, electronic or mechanical, including photocopying, recording or by any information storage and retrieval system, without prior permission in writing from the publisher.

Cover design: Luke Harris
Editor: Sarah Fallon

ISBN: 9781923116740 (pbk)
ISBN: 9781923116757 (ebk)

A catalogue record for this book is available from the National Library of Australia.

For All EAL Teachers
"Together, we are an ocean"
Ryūnosuke Akutagawa

ACKNOWLEDGEMENTS

This book is the result of five years of planning, robust discussions with English as an Additional Language/Dialect (EAL/D) teachers, and sifting through hundreds of model texts to find a "good fit" for a particular cohort of EAL/D students. Firstly, I would like to thank the late Arielle Foss-Ellis, my mentor who first introduced me to the pedagogy of theme based lessons during my time in a British International school. This was the foundation of my curiosity of how to use genre to teach EAL/D students.

I would also like to thank Helen Williams, my first mentor in an Australian Intensive English Centre (IEC) in Western Australia. Additionally, I would like to thank the amazing and dedicated EAL/D teachers at the IEC who collaborated and worked tirelessly to teach English to a group of newly arrived students. You supported, challenged, and encouraged me to further hone my genre based teaching skills.

I am also extremely grateful to Chris Pipka and all the teachers at the English Language Centre (ELC) in Victoria who encouraged and trusted me to create a genre based curriculum and moderation documents using the EAL/D continuum. Your patience and dedication of two years of trial and error taught me many skills that are now part of this book.

Finally, I want to thank Alicia Cohen at Amba Press for all her support and encouragement through some of my personal journeys while completing this creative process. Last but not least thank you Luke Harris for the exciting cover design and Sarah Fallon for your editing processes.

CONTENTS

Introduction

	Why this book?	7
	What is genre-based teaching?	7
	How does genre-based teaching help EAL/D students?	7
	How to use this book?	8

Part One — Beginning (Beginner Level)

Cover Page	Part 1 – Beginning/Beginner Level Explanation and Links to Australian Curriculum	10
Teacher's Notes	Genre 1 – What is a Procedure?	11
Text 1	Procedure – Simple Recipe – How to make pancakes?	12
	Reading and Viewing Activities	15
Teacher's Notes	Genre 1 – What is a Procedure?	17
Text 2	Procedure – Simple Instruction – How to make playdough?	18
	Reading and Viewing Activities	20
Teacher's Notes	Genre 2 – What is a Personal Recount?	23
Text 1	Personal Recount – All About Me	24
	Reading and Viewing Activities	25
Text 2	Personal Recount – My Daily Routine	30
	Reading and Viewing Activities	32
Teacher's Notes	Genre 3 – What is a Descriptive Report?	36
Text 1	Descriptive Report – Australian Animal	37
	Reading and Viewing Activities	38
Text 2	Descriptive Report – My Teacher	42
	Reading and Viewing Activities	44

Part Two – Emerging (Post Beginner Level)

Cover Page	Part 2 – Emerging/Post Beginner Level Explanation and Links to Australian Curriculum	49
Teacher's Notes	Genre 1 – What is a Comparative Report?	50
Text 1	Comparative Report – Comparing English and Arabic	51
Text 2	Comparative Report – Comparing Mammals and Reptiles	58
Teacher's Notes	Genre 2 – What is a Sequential Explanation?	65
Text 1	Sequential Explanation – Lifecycle of a Sunflower	66
Text 2	Sequential Explanation – Water Cycle	72
Teacher's Notes	Genre 3 – What is an Argument?	78
Text 1	Argument – Mobile Phones Should Be Allowed in Schools	78
Text 2	Argument – Is Homework Necessary?	87

Part 3 – Developing (Intermediate Level)

Cover Page	Part 3 – Developing/Intermediate Level Explanation and Links to Australian Curriculum	93
Teacher's Notes	Genre 1 – What is Historical Recount?	95
Text 1	Historical Recount – Ancient Egypt	96
Text 2	Historical recount – The First Fleet	105
Teacher's Notes	Genre 2 – What is a Descriptive Report?	113
Text 1	Descriptive Report – The Solar System	114
Text 2	Descriptive Report – Human Respiratory System	123
Teacher's Notes	Genre 3 – What is a Book Report?	130
Text 1	Book Report 1 – The Little Refugee	131
Text 2	Book Report 2 – The Rabbits	138

Part 4 – Consolidating (Advanced Level)

Cover Page	Part 4 – Consolidating/Advanced Level Explanation and Links to Australian Curriculum	147
Teacher's Notes	Genre 1 – What is a Science Report?	147
Text 1	Science Report – Electricity	148
Text 2	Science Report – Lifecycle of a bean plant	158
Teacher's Notes	Genre 2 – What is a Text Analysis?	168
Text 1	Text Analysis – Movie – Moana	169
Text 2	Text Analysis – Poem. 'The Road Not Taken' by Robert Frost	177
Teacher's Notes	Genre 3 – What is Language Analysis?	186
Text 1	Language Analysis – Blog on Climate Change	187
Text 2	Language Analysis – Youth Issues – Letter to Editor	199

Introduction

Why this book?

Model texts are an essential part of teaching writing. Hattie (2009) calls them "worked examples" and found that they have an effect size of 0.57. During my time as an English as an Additional Language/Dialect (EAL/D) curriculum leader and learning specialist, teachers would often approach me requesting support in finding or creating model texts. While creating a resource bank, I discovered that although there were many model texts out there, few were EAL/D specific or provided enough details for in-depth exploration and deconstruction.

This genre-based teacher's resource book with cross-curricular annotated model texts is designed for EAL/D teacher to:

- deliver engaging and meaningful worked examples.
- develop their students' writing and language skills across a range of genres.
- assist students to contextually deconstruct the texts at word, sentence, and text levels.
- support students to analyse structure, language features, and organisation of the different genres.
- experiment with functional grammar skills.

This book is designed to be flexible and adaptable to meet the needs of different classrooms and learners, ranging from beginner to advanced level EAL/D students. This resource book will be a valuable time saving tool for teachers as each genre is presented as a complete lesson that can be embedded into existing planning documents.

What is genre-based teaching?

- The teaching of language through various genres or types of texts.
- It focuses on teaching students how to analyse, understand, and produce different types of texts in order to develop their language skills.
- It develops abilities to communicate effectively in different situations and for different purposes.
- It provides opportunities to analyse the structure, language features, and organisation of different texts and genres, and to practise producing them in various contexts.
- It can be applied to different levels and types of language learning, from basic grammar and vocabulary to advanced writing and speaking skills.
- It helps students develop their language skills in a more integrated and meaningful way.
- It increases student motivation and engagement in the learning process.
- It can help students to become more effective communicators in a range of professional and personal contexts.

How does genre-based teaching help EAL/D students?

Using genre model texts is an effective way to teach writing skills because it provides EAL/D students with examples of how to structure and organise their writing in different genres or types of texts. Genre-based teaching can be particularly helpful for EAL/D students because it provides them with a framework for understanding and producing different types of texts in English. This approach helps EAL/D students to develop their language skills in a more integrated way, by teaching them how to use language effectively in different contexts and for different purposes. Additionally, genre-based teaching can benefit EAL/D students by:

- **Providing clear structure**: Genre model texts provide a clear structure for EAL/D students to follow when writing in a particular genre. This can help students to understand the expectations for the genre and to organise their ideas in a coherent way.
- **Building on prior knowledge**: By using familiar genres and texts from students' home languages and cultures, genre-based teaching can help EAL/D students to build on their prior knowledge and to transfer their existing skills to the new language.
- **Illustrating language features**: Genre model texts can also be used to highlight specific language features that are common to a particular genre, such as vocabulary, tone, and sentence structure. This can help students to understand how to use language effectively in different contexts.
- **Developing language skills**: Through the analysis and production of different genres, EAL/D students can develop their vocabulary, grammar, and discourse skills, as well as their ability to use language for different purposes.
- **Engaging students**: Using interesting and relevant genre model texts can engage EAL/D students in the writing process and motivate them to learn more about different genres. This can help to increase their confidence and interest for writing.
- **Supporting diverse learners**: Genre model texts can be particularly beneficial for EAL/D students, as they provide a clear structure and framework for writing in a particular genre. By following the structure of the model text, students can focus on generating ideas and developing their language skills.
- **Developing critical thinking**: Using genre model texts can also help to develop students' critical thinking skills, as they analyse and evaluate the structure, language features, and organisation of different texts.

How to use this book?

This book is meant to be a time saving tool that can be embedded in your planning document.

Before you do that, you may need to:

- Decide your EAL/D students' competency level.
- Identify the purpose of your lesson: This will help you to select the appropriate part, genre, and text from the book.
- Familiarise yourself with the genre: Read the teacher's note provided at the beginning of each genre. Analyse the structure, language features, and organisation of the selected texts. Identify the key writing skills, grammar, and vocabulary provided for each model text.
- Gather resources: Use the texts and activities from the book to prepare or gather additional resources.

During the lesson you may need to:

- Provide feedback: Provide continuous and meaningful feedback to students on their tasks. Use the annotated model texts in the book as examples to highlight areas for improvement and to show students how to improve their writing.

The tasks for each text are linked to the Teaching and Learning Cycle (Derewianka & Jones, 2016) that consist of:

Building the context or field	The **discussion questions** under each annotated text allow teachers to: • Create a safe space to discuss students' existing knowledge. • Begin building awareness and new knowledge of the genre.
Modelling the text (deconstruction)	The **annotated text** is used as a mentor text for the genre it represents and allows teachers to: • Focus on structure and language. • Explore how language is used to create meaning. To complement this, **the word and sentence level tasks** create additional opportunities to deconstruct the text and generate deeper understanding of vocabulary, grammar, and language features of a particular genre.
Guided practice (joint construction)	The **text level tasks** provide opportunities for teachers to: • Scaffold and share reading and writing skills with their students. • Embed cooperative learning strategies to allow student collaboration and discussion. • Jointly create a sample text for the genre.
Independent construction –	The **writing suggestion** at the end of each text give teachers options to: • Support students to produce their own text. • Provide one-on-one feedback. • Introduce the writing process – prewriting, drafting, revising, editing, publishing.

After the lesson you may need to:

- Evaluate progress: Evaluate the progress of your students in achieving the learning objectives and outcomes you identified at the beginning of the process. This can be a part of your formative assessment.

PART 1:
English as an Additional Language / Dialect (EAL/D) Beginner/Beginning Level

Who Are Beginner EAL/D Students?

Beginner EAL students have limited to no prior exposure to the English language. They come from diverse linguistic backgrounds and home languages. These students are at the earliest stage of their English language learning journey, and their needs and experiences can be quite distinct.

Challenges Faced by Beginner EAL/D Students

Beginner EAL/D students often face several challenges, such as:

- Limited Vocabulary: These students typically start with a small vocabulary, making it difficult to express themselves.
- Basic Grammar: Understanding English grammar rules and structures can be a significant hurdle.
- Cultural Adjustment: Adapting to a new culture and education system can also be overwhelming.

Strategies to Support Beginner EAL/D Students

To help beginner EAL/D students on their language acquisition journey, consider the following strategies:

- Create a Supportive Environment: Foster an inclusive and welcoming classroom atmosphere where students feel comfortable practicing English.
- Visual Aids and Contextual Learning: Use visuals, real-life examples, and hands-on activities to aid comprehension.
- Allow processing/wait time: This encourages students at this level to more confidently attempt speaking, reading and writing tasks.
- Select authentic materials: Connect with students' past and present needs and experiences.

Genres and some Australian Curriculum links for this level:

Genre	Topic	Australian Curriculum link
Procedure	Simple Recipe – How to make pancakes	using teacher's editing and conferencing including editing for word order, articles, prepositions and simple tenses. (ACEEA125)
	Simple Instructions – How to make paly dough	using visual information and home language or dialect to support understanding (ACEEA109)
Personal Recount	All About Me	using simple first-person recounts and descriptions (ACEEA121)
	My Daily Routine	using some written and oral text forms and grammatical structures, including the linear sequencing of events through the use of simple sentences, conjunctions, punctuation and paragraphs (ACEEA120)
Descriptive Report	Australian Animal – Kangaroos	retelling the gist and responding to texts and ideas considered in class (ACEEA112)
	My Teacher	using commonly used logographs, for example $, &, and abbreviations, for example Mr, Mrs (ACEEA124)

Part One – Beginner/Beginning Level – Procedure

Genre 1, Text 1

Teacher's Notes: What is a Procedure?

A procedure is a list of actions or steps that we need to make or do something. Examples of procedures include recipes, experiments, art and craft projects, directions, and games etc. Simple procedures are written as step-by-step guides with present tense verbs at the beginning of each step. In order to complete the procedure, we need to follow the steps in the correct order. They are factual texts although students could experiment with imaginary procedures such as making a magic spell. Procedures usually have "how to" titles to state their purpose and include a list of ingredients or tools that need to be prepared before beginning. Some procedures may include warnings and safety recommendations.

Features of a Procedure

- Written in clear and easy to understand language.
- Presented in a logical order.
- Include specific details and safety warnings if needed.
- List materials and tools needed.

Text 1 – Procedure – Simple Recipe

What is a recipe?

A recipe is a set of procedures to create or cook food. Simple recipes include a title, list of ingredients and their correct measurements, utensils, and step-by-step instructions on what to do. Professional recipes may include preparation and cooking times, number of servings, and nutritional information.

Genre 1 – Procedure – Simple Recipe
How to Make Pancakes

Word Bank

	What I need	
flour	2 cups	
eggs	2	
milk	1 cup	
bowl and spoon	1 each	
pan	1	
sugar	½ cup	
lemon	1	

Unlocking Genre 12

What I DO	
sift	
break	
pour	
mix	
cook	
cut	
squeeze	
sprinkle	

Model Text – Annotated for whole class discussion

What you need:	
Ingredients	Utensils
2 cups of flour 2 eggs 1 cup of milk ½ cup of sugar 1 lemon	A bowl A spoon A pan

How to make Pancakes	Title
1. Sift the flour into the bowl. 2. Break the eggs into the bowl. 3. Pour the milk. 4. Mix the ingredients with a spoon. 5. Cook the pancake. 6. Cut and squeeze lemon juice over the pancake. 7. Sprinkle some sugar on the pancake. 8. Serve and enjoy.	Verbs at the beginning of the sentences. Numbers make it easy to follow step-by step. Capital letters and full stops.

Discussion questions:

1. Where do we write the title?
2. Why does our recipe need a title?
3. Why does the recipes have numbers?
4. Can we start anywhere we want? Why?
5. What do we call the words at the beginning of each instruction?
6. What do verbs tell us?
7. What tense are the verbs in? Why?
8. Where can we get or buy the ingredients?
9. Why does the recipe tell us the amount of each ingredient?
10. Why do we need to use capital letters and full stops?

Model Text – Non-Annotated

1. Sift the flour into the bowl.
2. Break the eggs into the bowl.
3. Pour the milk.
4. Mix the ingredients with a spoon.
5. Cook the pancake.
6. Cut and squeeze lemon juice over the pancake
7. Sprinkle some sugar on the pancake.
8. Serve and enjoy.

Reading and Viewing Activities

A: Word Level

1. List all the verbs you can see.

```
┌─────────────────────────────────────────────────────┐
│                                                     │
│                                                     │
│                                                     │
│                                                     │
└─────────────────────────────────────────────────────┘
```

2. The verbs are written in the _____ tense because _____.

B: Sentence Level

Answer the questions using complete sentences.

1. Where are we adding the flour, eggs, and milk?
   _____
2. What are we making?
   _____
3. Do you think this pancake will be tasty? Why?
   _____

Fill in the blanks with the correct words from the recipe.

We need _____, _____, and _____ to make pancakes. We mix everything

in a _____ and cook the pancakes in a _____. We can sprinkle _____ and _____

on the pancakes before we _____ them.

C: Text Level

	Rewrite the instructions in the correct word order. Don't forget your CAPITAL letters and full stops.	Order the instructions using numbers.
milk the pour		
some sprinkle sugar the pancake on		
and serve enjoy		
the cook pancake		
bowl sift the flour into the		
eggs break bowl the into		
ingredients mix a with spoon the		
pancake some sprinkle on sugar the		

Functional Grammar

	Describe	What?	Extra Information
the	white, soft	flour	that you measured
the		bowl	
the		eggs	
the		milk	
the		ingredients	
a		spoon	
the		pancake	
		lemon juice	
some		sugar	

D: Writing

Write your own instructions. Use the table below to make your nouns more interesting before you write your instructions.

How to cook Scrambled Eggs

What I need:	Verbs:
eggs, milk, butter, bowl, pan	break, add, mix, cook, enjoy

	Describe	What?	Extra Information
the		eggs	
the		milk	
the		butter	
a		bowl	

Part One – Beginner/Beginning Level – Procedure

Genre 1, Text 2

Teacher's Notes: What is a Procedure?

A procedure is a list of actions or steps that we need to make or do something. Examples of procedures include recipes, experiments, art and craft projects, directions, and games etc. Simple procedures are written as step-by-step guides with present tense verbs at the beginning of each step. In order to complete the procedure, we need to follow the steps in the correct order. They are factual texts although students could experiment with imaginary procedures such as making a magic spell. Procedures usually have "how to" titles to state their purpose and include a list of ingredients or tools that need to be prepared before beginning. Some procedures may include warnings and safety recommendations.

Features of a Procedure

- Written in clear and easy to understand language.
- Presented in a logical order.
- Include specific details and safety warnings if needed.
- List materials and tools needed.

Text 2 – Procedure – Simple Instructions

How to make playdough?

Simple instructions can be used to help students complete a short art and craft project or make something in the classroom. Simple instructions include a title, list of materials and their correct measurements, tools, and step-by-step instructions on what to do.

Genre 1 – Procedure – Simple Instructions
How to Make Playdough

Word Bank

What I NEED		
	1 cup	
salt		
oil	½ table spoon	
warm water	¼ cup	
food colouring	1 drop	
bowl	1	
chopping board	1	
plastic cup	1	

What I DO	
mix	
pour	
add	
knead	

Model Text – Annotated for whole class discussion

What you need:	
Material	**Utensils**
1 cup of flour	A bowl
½ cup of salt	A chopping board
½ table spoon of oil	
½ cup warm water	
1 drop of food colouring	

How to make Playdough ←	Title
1. Mix the flour and salt in the bowl. 2. Pour the warm water and oil into the plastic cup. 3. Add the food colouring into the water and mix. 4. Pour the coloured water into the bowl. 5. Mix everything. 6. Knead on the chopping board. 7. Enjoy playing with your playdough.	Verbs at the beginning of the sentences. Numbers make it easy to follow step-by step. Capital letters and full stops.

Discussion questions:

1. Where do we write the title?
2. Why do our instructions need a title?
3. Why do the instructions have numbers?
4. Can we start anywhere we want? Why?
5. What do we call the words at the beginning of each instruction?
6. What do verbs tell us?
7. What tense are the verbs in? Why?
8. Where can we get or buy the materials?
9. Why does the instruction tell us the amount of each material?
10. Why do we need to use capital letters and full stops?

Model Text – Non-Annotated

1. Mix the flour and salt in the bowl.
2. Pour the warm water and oil into the plastic cup.
3. Add the food colouring into the water and mix.
4. Pour the coloured water into the bowl.
5. Mix everything.
6. Knead on the chopping board.
7. Enjoy playing with your playdough.

Reading and Viewing Activities

A: Word Level

1. List all the verbs you can see.

2. The verbs are written in the _____ tense because _____.

B: Sentence Level

Answer the questions using complete sentences.

1. What are we doing before we add the warm water?
   _____
2. What are we adding to the warm water?
   _____
3. Do you think you can teach your family how to make playdough?
   _____

Fill in the blanks with the correct words from the instruction.

The five ingredients we need to make playdough are:

1. _____
2. _____
3. _____
4. _____
5. _____

We mix everything in a _____ and _____ on a _____.

C: Text Level

Rearrange the instructions in the correct order.

	Rewrite the instructions in the correct word order. Don't forget your CAPITAL letters and full stops.	Order the instructions using numbers.
chopping board on the knead		
the mix and colouring the add food water into		
flour bowl the and salt the in mix		
with enjoy playdough your playing		
water cup pour plastic oil warm the into and the		
everything mix		
Water the bowl the coloured into pour		

Functional Grammar

	Describe	What?	Extra Information
the	white, soft	flour	in the bowl
the		salt	
the		water	
the		food colouring	
the		cup	
a		chopping board	
the		playdough	
the		oil	

D: Writing

Write your own instructions. Use the table below to make your nouns more interesting before you write your instructions.

How to make playdough rock faces

What I need:	Verbs:
playdough, googly eyes, rock	add, knead, enjoy, shape

	Describe	What?	Extra Information
the		playdough	
the		rock	
the		googly eyes	

Part One – Beginner/Beginning Level – Personal Recount

Genre 2, Text 1

Teacher's Notes: What is a Personal Recount?

A personal recount retells an event or experience from the writer's own perspective. The purpose of a personal recount is to share a personal experience with others, often with the aim of entertaining, informing or reflecting on the experience.

Personal recounts can take many forms, including everyday experiences, narratives, memoirs, diaries, or letters. They often include details of the writer's activities, feelings, thoughts, and reactions to the experience, as well as descriptions of the setting and other people involved.

When writing a personal recount, it is important to use descriptive language to help the reader visualise the experience and to convey the emotions and thoughts of the writer. It can also be helpful to use chronological order to structure the recount and to use transitions to move smoothly between different parts of the story.

Personal recounts can be a valuable tool for developing writing skills in English as an Additional Language/Dialect (EAL/D) students. They encourage students to reflect on their own experiences and to use language effectively to communicate their ideas and feelings to others. They can also be a powerful way to build empathy and understanding between students of different cultural backgrounds, as they allow readers to step into the shoes of the writer and see the world from their perspective.

Features of a Personal Recount

- First Person Point of View
- Chronological Order
- Descriptive Language: This can include sensory details such as sights, sounds, and smells.
- Personal Reflection: Personal recounts often include personal reflections or thoughts about the events being recounted. This can help the reader understand the writer's perspective on the events.
- Dialogue: Personal recounts may include dialogue to help bring the events to life and give the reader a sense of the conversations that took place.
- Emotions and Feelings: Personal recounts can include emotions and feelings of the writer. This can help the reader understand the impact that the events had on the writer.

Text 1 – Personal Recount

All About Me

Personal recounts can be used to help EAL/D students share information about themselves. They are effective ice-breakers and can help with overcoming initial shyness and disengagement.

Genre 2 – Personal Recount
All about Me

Word Bank

curly hair	
birthday	
village	
family	
airplane	
scared	
happy	
Long braids	
nurse	
grandmother	

Model Text – Annotated for whole class discussion

All About Me (Title – tells us what we are recounting)	
Paragraph 1	
My name is Amani.	Start with your name.
I am twelve years old.	How old are you?
I am from Sudan.	Where are you from?
I was born in my village in Sudan.	Where were you born?
My birthday is on 20th of March.	When is your birthday?
In Sudan, I went to the school in my village. All my brothers, sisters, and cousins went there too.	Did you go to school in your home country?
We learned English and Mathematics. I was a good student. I was also good at running, and won many prizes. I liked learning English and playing soccer with my friends.	What did you do at school there?
Paragraph 2	
I came to Australia in 2022, and I started school at a Language School to learn English.	When did you come to Australia? Where did you go to school in Australia?
I miss my school in Sudan but I like my school in Australia because the teachers are very kind.	Do you miss your school in your home country? How do you feel about school in Australia?
There are six people in my family. They are my dad, my mum, my two brothers, my sister, and me. I am the youngest.	Say something about your family.
All of us came to Australia because people were fighting in Sudan and it was not safe for us to stay there.	Why did you leave your country?
We came to Australia by airplane. It was my first time on an airplane. I was scared but also happy.	How did you come to Australia?
Paragraph 3	
In Sudan, I had short, black, curly hair but now I have long braids.	Say something about yourself.
When I was in Sudan, I loved to eat Mullah. It is like a meat curry. In Australia, my favourite food is rice with chicken.	Your favourite food.
When I was young, I wanted to be a teacher because I like to teach children. Now, I think I want to be a nurse because I can help people.	What did you want to be when you grow up? Why? Do you still want to do the same thing when you grow up?
During my school holidays in Sudan, I visited my grandmother. She lived In another village. I liked listening to her stories.	What do you want to do during the school holiday?
I want my teacher to know that I feel happy when I am learning English.	One thing you want your teacher to know about you?
VERBS are in the present tense. VERBS are in the past tense when you are writing about what happened in Sudan.	

Discussion questions:

1. Where do we write the title?
2. Why does our story need a title?
3. Why does our story have paragraphs?
4. How do we start to write "All About Me"? Why?
5. What different tenses are the verbs in? Why?
6. What is a paragraph? How many paragraphs are there?
7. Why do we need to use capital letters and full stops?
8. When do we use commas? Why?

Model Text – Non-Annotated

All About Me

My name is Amani. I am twelve years old. I am from Sudan. I was born in my village in Sudan. My birthday is on 20th of March. In Sudan, I went to the school in my village. All my brothers, sisters, and cousins went there too. We learned English and Mathematics. I was a good student. I was also good at running, and won many prizes. I liked learning English and playing soccer with my friends.

I came to Australia in 2022, and I started school at a Language School to learn English. I miss my school in Sudan but I like my school in Australia because the teachers are very kind. There are six people in my family. They are my dad, my mum, my two brothers, my sister, and me. I am the youngest. All of us came to Australia because people were fighting in Sudan and it was not safe for us to stay there. We came to Australia by airplane. It was my first time on an airplane. I was scared but also happy.

In Sudan, I had short, black, curly hair but now I have long braids. When I was in Sudan, I loved to eat Mullah. It is like a meat curry. In Australia, my favourite food is rice with chicken. When I was young, I wanted to be a teacher's because I like to teach children. Now, I think I want to be a nurse because I can help people. During my school holidays in Sudan, I visited my grandmother. She lived in another village. I liked listening to her stories. I want my teacher to know that I feel happy when I am learning English.

Reading and Viewing Activities

A: Word Level

1. List all the verbs you can see.

   [   ]

2. The verbs are written in the _____ and _____ tenses because _____.

B: Sentence Level

Answer the questions using complete sentences.

1. Where is Amani from?
   _____
2. What did Amani do well when she was at school in Sudan?
   _____
3. How did Amani come to Australia?
   _____

Fill in the blanks with the correct words from the story.

My name is Amani. I am _____ years old. I am from _____. I was born in my _____ in Sudan. My _____ is on 20th of March. In Sudan, I went to the school in my _____. All my brothers, sisters, and _____ went there too. We learned _____ and Mathematics. I was a good student. I was also good at _____, and won many _____. I _____ learning English and playing _____ with my friends.

I came to _____ in 2022, and I started school at a Language School to learn _____. I miss my school in _____ but I like my school in Australia because the teachers are very _____. There are six people in my _____. They are my dad, my mum, my _____ brothers, my sister, and me. I am the _____. All of us came to Australia _____ people were fighting in Sudan and it was not _____ for us to stay there. We came to Australia by _____. It was my first time on an airplane. I was _____ but also happy.

In Sudan, I had short, _____, curly hair but now I have long _____. When I was in Sudan, I _____ to eat Mullah. It is like a _____ curry. In Australia, my _____ food is rice with chicken. When I was young, I wanted to be a _____ because I like to teach _____. Now, I think I want to be a _____ because I can help people. During my school holidays in Sudan, I visited my _____. She lived in another village. I liked _____ to her stories. I want my teacher to know that I feel _____ when I am learning English.

C: Text Level

Write TRUE or FALSE. If it is FALSE, write the correct answer – two examples have been completed for you.

Amani is from Sudan.	TRUE	
Amani is older than her sister.	FALSE	Amani is the youngest.
Amani does not miss her school in Sudan.		
Amani has many brothers.		
Amani is not happy when she is learning English.		
Amani was happy to be on the airplane.		
Amani enjoys playing soccer.		
In Australia, Amani likes to eat rice.		
Amani does not like running.		
There are six people in Amani's family.		
Amani left Sudan because she did not like the school there.		

Functional Grammar

	Describe	What?	Extra Information
my	black, curly	hair	is beautiful
		eyes	
		brother	
		sister	
		teacher's	

D: Writing

Write your own story. Use the questions from the table below to help you.

Paragraph 1
What is your name.
How old are you?
When is your birthday?
Where are you from?
Did you go to school in your home country?
What did you do at school in your home country?
Paragraph 2
When did you come to Australia?
How did you come to Australia?
How did you feel when you were coming to Australia?
Why did your family leave your home country?
Say something about your family.
Paragraph 3
Describe something about yourself when you were in your home country.
What was your favourite food in your home country?
Do you have a different favourite food in Australia?
What did you want to be when you grew up? Why?
What did you do during the school holidays in your home country?
One thing you want your teacher to know about you?

Part One – Beginner/Beginning Level – Personal Recount

Genre 2, Text 2

Teacher's Notes: What is a Personal Recount?

A personal recount retells an event or experience from the writer's own perspective. The purpose of a personal recount is to share a personal experience with others, often with the aim of entertaining, informing or reflecting on the experience.

Personal recounts can take many forms, including everyday experiences, narratives, memoirs, diaries, or letters. They often include details of the writer's activities, feelings, thoughts, and reactions to the experience, as well as descriptions of the setting and other people involved.

When writing a personal recount, it is important to use descriptive language to help the reader visualise the experience and to convey the emotions and thoughts of the writer. It can also be helpful to use chronological order to structure the recount and to use transitions to move smoothly between different parts of the story.

Personal recounts can be a valuable tool for developing writing skills in English as an Additional Language/Dialect (EAL/D) students. They encourage students to reflect on their own experiences and to use language effectively to communicate their ideas and feelings to others. They can also be a powerful way to build empathy and understanding between students of different cultural backgrounds, as they allow readers to step into the shoes of the writer and see the world from their perspective.

Features of a Personal Recount

- First Person Point of View
- Chronological Order
- Descriptive Language: This can include sensory details such as sights, sounds, and smells.
- Personal Reflection: Personal recounts often include personal reflections or thoughts about the events being recounted. This can help the reader understand the writer's perspective on the events.
- Dialogue: Personal recounts may include dialogue to help bring the events to life and give the reader a sense of the conversations that took place.
- Emotions and Feelings: Personal recounts can include emotions and feelings of the writer. This can help the reader understand the impact that the events had on the writer.

Text 2 – Personal Recount – My Daily Routine

My Daily Routine – What I Did Yesterday

Personal recounts can be used to help EAL/D students share information about themselves. They are effective ice-breakers and can help with overcoming initial shyness and disengagement.

Genre 2 – Personal Recount
My Daily Routine – What I Did Yesterday

Word Bank

	Picture of		Picture of
AM		bus	
PM		classroom	
woke up		played	
got up		tv	
brushed teeth		homework	
took a shower		park	
put on uniform		make dinner	
breakfast		went to bed	

Unlocking Genre 31

My Daily Routine – What I Did Yesterday

Model Text – Annotated for whole class discussion

Time (Heading)	What I did (Heading – tells us what is in this column)	
7:00 AM	I woke up	What time did you wake up?
7:10 AM	I got up.	What did you do after you get up?
7:15 AM	I brushed my teeth and took a shower.	
7:30 AM	I put on my uniform.	
7:45 AM	I ate breakfast.	
8:00 AM	I went to school by bus.	How did you go to school?
8:45 AM	I went to my classroom.	What did you do at school?
9:00 AM	I had my first lesson.	
10:45 AM	I had recess. I went out and played with my friends.	
11:00 AM	I went back to my class.	
12:30 PM	I had lunch and played with my friends.	
3:00 PM	I finished school and went home.	
3:30 PM	I watched TV.	What did you do after you got home from school?
4:30 PM	I did my homework.	
5:30 PM	I went to the park and played with my friends.	
6:30 PM	I helped my mum to make dinner.	
7:30 PM	I had a shower and ate dinner with my family.	
8:30 PM	I watched TV with my family.	
9:30 PM	I went to bed.	When did you go to bed?
Past tense		

Discussion questions:

1. What is the difference between "woke up" and "got up"?
2. Let's talk about AM and PM.
3. What are some of the things that we do in the morning?
4. What are some of the things that we do at school?
5. What are some of the things that we do after school?
6. Why do we call this "My Daily Routine"?
7. How is your daily routine different on the weekends?
8. What did you do last weekend?

My Daily Routine – What I Did Yesterday
Model Text – Non-Annotated

Time	What I did
7:00 AM	I woke up
7:10 AM	I got up.
7:15 AM	I brushed my teeth and took a shower.
7:30 AM	I put on my uniform.
7:45 AM	I ate breakfast.
8:00 AM	I went to school by bus.
8:45 AM	I went to my classroom.
9:00 AM	I had my first lesson.
10:45 AM	I had recess. I went out and played with my friends.
11:00 AM	I went back to my class.
12:30 PM	I had lunch and played with my friends.
3:00 PM	I finished school and went home.
3:30 PM	I watched TV.
4:30 PM	I did my homework.
5:30 PM	I went to the park and played with my friends.
6:30 PM	I helped my mum to make dinner.
7:30 PM	I had a shower and ate dinner with my family.
8:30 PM	I watched TV with my family.
9:30 PM	I went to bed.

Reading and Viewing Activities
A: Word Level

1. List all the verbs you can see.

2. The verbs are written in the _____ tense because _____.

B: Sentence Level
Answer the questions using complete sentences.

1. When does PM start?
    _____
2. List three things that happened in AM.
    a. _____
    b. _____
    c. _____
3. List three things that happened in PM.
    a. _____
    b. _____
    c. _____
4. What happened before 7:30AM?
    _____
5. What happened after 5:30 PM?
    _____

Unlocking Genre

Complete these sentences using the daily routine in table:

1. Before I put on my uniform, I _____.
2. After I ate my breakfast, I _____.
3. After recess, I _____.
4. _____ before I did my homework.
5. _____ after I did my homework.

C: Text Level

Rearrange the sentences in the correct order.

_____ I ate dinner with my family.
_____ I put on my uniform.
_____ I woke up.
_____ I went to bed.
_____ I ate breakfast.
_____ I did my homework.
_____ I went to my classroom.
_____ I helped my mum make dinner.
_____ I had lunch and played with my friends.
_____ I went to the park and played with my friends.

Functional Grammar
Highlight all the nouns.

I put on my uniform. I ate breakfast. I went to school by bus. I went to my classroom. I played with my friends. I did my homework. I helped my mum to make dinner.

Write the nouns in the table below and add descriptions. One example has been done for you:

	Describe	What?	Extra Information
a	delicious	dinner	cooked by my mother.

D: Writing

Write your own. Use the table below to help you.

Title	What I did on Sunday
Time	What I did
7:00 AM	
7:10 AM	
7:15 AM	
7:30 AM	
7:45 AM	
8:00 AM	
8:45 AM	
9:00 AM	
10:45 AM	
11:00 AM	
12:30 PM	
3:00 PM	
3:30 PM	
4:30 PM	
5:30 PM	
6:30 PM	
7:30 PM	
8:30 PM	
9:30 PM	

Part One – Beginner/Beginning Level – Descriptive Report

Genre 3, Text 1

Teacher's Notes: What is a Descriptive Report?

A descriptive report aims to describe an object, person, place, event, or animal in detail. It is a non-fiction and factual description of the chosen subject.

Descriptive reports can include scientific reports, field reports, observation reports, and case studies. They often include detailed descriptions of the physical characteristics, properties, and behaviour of the subject being described.

When writing a descriptive report, it is important to organise the information in a logical and coherent way, using headings, subheadings, images, and transitions to guide the reader through the report.

For English as an Additional Language/Dialect (EAL/D) students, descriptive reports can be a valuable tool for developing observation and analytical skills, as well as for communicating scientific or technical information in a clear and accessible way. They are an effective way to allow objective observations and build academic writing skills.

Features of a Descriptive Report

- Sensory details – describing what we can see, hear, smell, taste, and feel.
- Clearly and logically organised – may include heading, sub-headings, images with captions, etc.
- Objective language – more facts, less personal opinions.
- Language features – adjectives and adverbs to create more depth.

Text 1 – Descriptive Report – Australian Animal

Kangaroos

Researching Australian animals and writing about them can help EAL/D students connect with their current environment. Writing simple descriptive reports at the beginner level allows students to experiment with fundamental skills for academic and non-fiction work.

Genre 3 – Descriptive Report
Kangaroos

Word Bank

Note

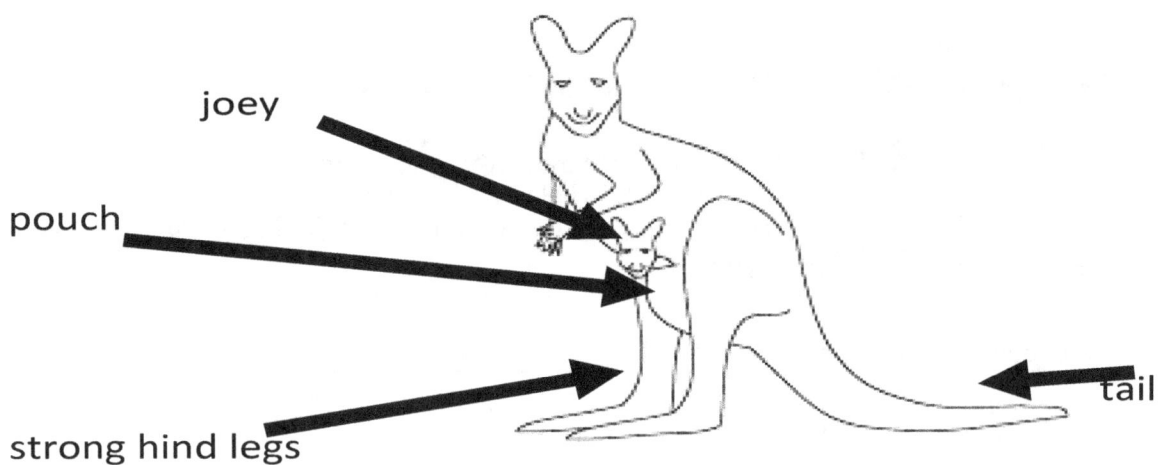

Model Text – Annotated for whole class discussion

Kangaroos (Title -we use the plural form because we are writing about all kangaroos)

What are kangaroos?
(Sub-heading or Paragraph Title – tells us what the paragraph is about)

(The first sentence answers the question in the sub-heading) Kangaroos are mammals that give birth to their babies. They are found in Australia and Papua New Guinea. Kangaroos are also called marsupials because they carry their babies in their pouches. Baby kangaroos are called joeys. They are wild animals that live in the bush.

Verbs in the present tense – are, give, carry, live
Verbs in the passive voice – are found, are called
Pronouns to replace kangaroos, joeys – They/their

What do kangaroos have?
(Sub-heading or Paragraph Title – tells us what the paragraph is about)

(The first sentence answers the question in the sub-heading) Kangaroos have very strong hind legs and long tails. Their strong legs and tails help them to jump and move. They have brown, red, or grey fur on their backs and white fur on the stomachs. (Additional information that answer the question in the sub-heading)

Verbs in the present tense – have, jump
Pronoun to replace kangaroos – they

How do kangaroos live?
(Sub-heading or Paragraph Title – tells us what the paragraph is about)

(The first sentence answers the question in the sub-heading) Kangaroos live in family groups. This helps the group to share food and water. These groups are called mobs.

Kangaroos live in groups called mobs. (Picture with a caption)

Verbs in the present tense – live, helps
Verbs in the passive voice – are called

What do kangaroos eat?

Kangaroos are herbivores. They eat plants, leaves, and grass.

Interesting facts about kangaroos
- They cannot move backwards.
- They can live on very little water.
- Female kangaroos can move faster than male kangaroos.

Discussion questions
- What does the word **they** replace?
- What are the sub-headings? What do they tell you?

Unlocking Genre 38

Discussion questions:
1. Where do we write the title?
2. What do we write at the top of each paragraph?
3. How do sub-headings help us?
4. Why do you think we sometimes use 'they or their' instead of kangaroos or joeys again?
5. What are we thinking about when we write the first sentence of each paragraph?

Model Text – Non-Annotated

Kangaroos

What are kangaroos?
Kangaroos are mammals that give birth to their babies. They are found in Australia and Papua New Guinea. Kangaroos are also called marsupials because they carry their babies in their pouches. Baby kangaroos are called joeys. They are wild animals that live in the bush.

What do kangaroos have?
Kangaroos have very strong hind legs and long tails. Their strong legs and tails help them to jump and move. They have brown, red, or grey fur on their backs and white fur on the stomachs.

How do kangaroos live?
Kangaroos live in family groups. This helps the group to share food and water. These groups are called mobs.

Kangaroos live in groups called mobs.

What do kangaroos eat?
Kangaroos are herbivores. They eat plants, leaves, and grass.

Interesting facts about kangaroos
- They cannot move backwards.
- They can live on very little water.
- Female kangaroos can move faster than male kangaroos.

Reading and Viewing Activities

A: Word Level

1. List all the verbs you can see.

2. The verbs are written in the _____ tense because _____.
3. List all the nouns you can see.

4. What are the words we use to replace some of the nouns? _____
5. What do we call the words we use to replace the nouns? _____
6. Why is the title in plural? _____

Unlocking Genre 39

B: Sentence Level

Answer the questions using complete sentences.

1. Where can we find kangaroos?
   _____
2. Why are kangaroos called marsupials?
   _____
3. What parts of the body help kangaroos jump and move?
   _____
4. Why do you think living in family groups helps kangaroos with getting food and water?
   _____
5. What do we call animals that eat plants, leaves, and grass?
   _____
6. Why do you think kangaroos cannot move backwards?
   _____

Complete the information needed in the table below.

Title:	What does the title tell you?
Sub-heading one:	What is this paragraph about?
Sub-heading two:	What is this paragraph about?
Sub-heading three:	What is this paragraph about?
Sub-heading four:	What is this paragraph about?
Sub-heading five:	What is this paragraph about?

C: Text Level

Write TRUE or FALSE. If it is FALSE, write the correct answer – two examples have been completed for you.

Kangaroos give birth to their babies.	TRUE	
We can find kangaroos in all the countries in the world.	FALSE	Kangaroos are found in Australia and Papua New Guinea.
Marsupials have pouches where they carry babies.		
Baby kangaroos are called mobs.		
We can keep kangaroos as pets.		
Kangaroos have strong hind legs.		
Kangaroos have fur on their stomachs.		
Kangaroos live alone.		
Kangaroos eat meat.		
Female kangaroos move faster than male kangaroos.		

Functional Grammar

	Describe	What?	Extra Information
the	big, tall	kangaroo	is in the bush.
		joey	
		grass	
		fur	
		family	

D: Writing

Pick an animal and write a short report. Use the table below to help you.

Title:	Name of the animal you have chosen.
Sub-heading one:	What are _____?
Sub-heading two:	What do _____ have?
Sub-heading three:	What do _____ eat?
Sub-heading four:	How do _____ live?
Sub-heading five:	Three interesting facts about _____.

Part One – Beginner/Beginning Level – Descriptive Report

Genre 2, Text 2

Teacher's Notes: What is a Descriptive Report?

A descriptive report aims to describe an object, person, place, event, or animal in detail. It is a non-fiction and factual description of the chosen subject.

Descriptive reports can include scientific reports, field reports, observation reports, and case studies. They often include detailed descriptions of the physical characteristics, properties, and behaviour of the subject being described.

When writing a descriptive report, it is important to organise the information in a logical and coherent way, using headings, subheadings, images, and transitions to guide the reader through the report.

For English as an Additional Language/Dialect (EAL/D) students, descriptive reports can be a valuable tool for developing observation and analytical skills, as well as for communicating scientific or technical information in a clear and accessible way. They are an effective way to allow objective observations and build academic writing skills.

Features of a Descriptive Report

- Sensory details – describing what we can see, hear, smell, taste, and feel.
- Clearly and logically organised – may include heading, sub-headings, images with captions, etc.
- Objective language – more facts, less personal opinions.
- Language features – adjectives and adverbs to create more depth.

Text 2 – Descriptive Report

My Teacher

Observing, interviewing, and writing about their teachers can help EAL/D students connect with their new school environment. Writing simple descriptive reports at the beginner level allows students to experiment with fundamental skills for academic and non-fiction work.

Genre 3 – Descriptive Report
My Teacher

Word Bank

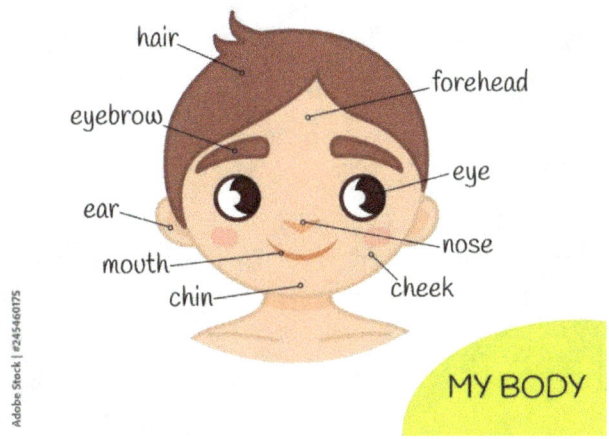

Name	Ms. Nathan
Job	English teacher
Hair	brown and curly
Favourite colour	red
Favourite food	rice and vegetables
Hobbies	reading and shopping
Fiction	From my imagination
Non-fiction	Real facts

Model Text – Annotated for whole class discussion

My Teacher (Title – tells us who we are describing)

Paragraph 1		
My teacher's name is Ms. Nathan.	Teacher's name	We use 's when we want to show that something belongs to someone. Verbs are in the present tense because we are writing about something that is true now.
She is tall and has brown, curly hair. She has brown eyes and wears glasses.	Describe – tall or short, colour and type of hair, glasses, make-up etc.	Verbs are in the present tense because we are writing about something that is true now. We use adjectives to describe nouns.
She has a red car because her favourite colour is red.	Favourite colour. What do they own in this colour?	Verbs are in the present tense because we are writing about something that is true now. We use adjectives to describe nouns.
She likes to eat rice and vegetables. She drinks a lot of water.	Favourite food and drink.	Verbs are in the present tense because we are writing about something that is true now. We do not add 's' to the verb after the word 'to'.

Unlocking Genre 44

Ms. Nathan likes reading and shopping when she is on holiday.	Hobbies. What do they like to do in their free time?	Verbs are in the present tense because we are writing about something that is true now.
Paragraph 2		
Ms. Nathan likes to use songs and interesting stories to teach us English.	What do they teach? How do they teach the subject?	Verbs are in the present tense because we are writing about something that is true now. We use adjectives to describe nouns. We do not add 's' to the verb after the word 'to'.
We learn the sounds of the letters so we can read and spell new English words. We move our hands and mouths to remember the sounds. This is a lot of fun. We talk with our friends to help each other when we are reading and writing. Ms. Nathan uses real things and pictures to help us understand new words.	How do we learn the subject? How does the teacher help us understand what we are learning?	Verbs are in the present tense because we are writing about something that is true now. We use adjectives to describe nouns. We do not add 's' to the verb after the word 'to'.
Paragraph 3		
I like my teacher because she is kind and always helps us when we are at school. She does not get angry if we ask questions. She likes to be a teacher and enjoys teaching us. We enjoy learning English in Ms. Nathan's class.	Why do you like your teacher?	Verbs are in the present tense because we are writing about something that is true now. We use adjectives to describe nouns.

Discussion questions:

1. Where do we write the title?
2. How do we know that we are starting a new paragraph? Are we writing about the same thing in each new paragraph?
3. How does the word bank help us write our report?
4. Are we writing a fiction or non-fiction text?
5. What are facts that we have included in the first paragraph?
6. What can we do if we want to know some things about our teacher?
7. Can we use the same ideas to write about a friend?

Model Text – Non-Annotated

My teacher's name is Ms. Nathan. She is tall and has brown, curly hair. She has brown eyes and wears glasses. She teaches us English. She has a red car because her favourite colour is red. She likes to eat rice and vegetables. She drinks a lot of water. Ms. Nathan likes reading and shopping when she is on holiday.

Ms. Nathan likes to use songs and interesting stories to teach us English. We learn the sounds of the letters so we can read and spell new English words. We move our hands and mouths to remember the sounds. This is a lot of fun. We talk with our friends to help each other when we are reading and writing. Ms. Nathan uses real things and pictures to help us understand new words.

I like my teacher because she is kind and always helps us when we are at school. She does not get angry if we ask questions. She likes to be a teacher and enjoys teaching us. We enjoy learning English in Ms. Nathan's class.

Reading and Viewing Activities

A: Word Level

1. List all the verbs you can see.

2. The verbs are written in the _____ tense because _____.
3. List all the nouns you can see.

4. List all the words we use to describe the nouns.

5. What do we call the words we use to describe the nouns? _____

B: Sentence Level

Answer the questions using complete sentences.

1. What is the teacher's name?
   _____
2. What words has the writer used to describe the teacher's hair? Add two more words of your own.
   _____
3. Why do you think the teacher wears glasses?
   _____
4. How does Ms. Nathan make her lessons more interesting?
   _____
5. Why do you think it is important to learn the sounds of letters?
   _____
6. List two reasons why the writer likes their teacher.
   _____

Add your own adjectives to make the sentences below more interesting.

She likes to eat vegetables.	
She drinks a lot of water.	
Ms. Nathan is a teacher.	
Ms. Nathan likes to use songs to teach us English.	
Ms. Nathan uses pictures to help us understand new words.	
She does not get angry if we ask questions.	

C: Text Level

Fill in the blanks with your own words or phrases. Do not copy from the text. The first one has been done for you.

My teacher's name is <u>Mr. Hammond</u>. He is _____ and has _____, _____ hair. He has _____ eyes and wears glasses. He teaches us _____. He has a _____ car because her favourite colour is _____. He likes to eat _____. He drinks a lot of _____.

Mr. Hammond likes _____ when he is on holiday.

Mr. Hammond likes to use _____ to teach us _____. We learn _____ so we can _____ new _____. Mr. Hammond uses _____ to help us understand new words.

I like my teacher because he is _____. He does not get angry if we ask questions. He likes to be a teacher and enjoys teaching us.

Functional Grammar

	Describe	What?	Extra Information
the	tall	teacher	is standing in the classroom.
		hair	
		eyes	
		glasses	
		car	
		vegetables	
		songs	
		friends	
		pictures	

D: Writing

Choose ONE friend. Use the table below to ask them questions. Write a short report about your friend.

Name	
Age	
Hair	
Eyes	
Height	
Favourite colour	
Favourite food	
Hobbies	
Draw a picture of your friend.	

PART 2:
English as an Additional Language / Dialect (EAL/D) Post Beginner/Emerging Level

Who Are Post Beginner/Emerging EAL/D Students?

Post Beginner/Emerging EAL/D students have made some progress in their English language acquisition journey and are beginning to develop understanding and application of the English language in their daily lives. They are beginning to move beyond the beginner stage of language acquisition. They have developed a foundational understanding of English but are still working on honing their language skills to achieve fluency.

Challenges Faced by Emerging EAL/D Students

Post Beginner/Emerging EAL/D students face a set of distinct challenges as they progress in their language acquisition journey:

- Expanding Vocabulary: Building a more extensive vocabulary to express complex ideas and thoughts.
- Advanced Grammar: Mastering more intricate grammar rules and sentence structures.
- Academic Language: Developing the language skills necessary to excel in academic settings.

Strategies to Support Emerging EAL/D Students

- Encourage Self-expression: Create opportunities for students to express themselves using their home languages through small group discussions.
- Provide Feedback: Offer constructive feedback on targeted grammar and structure using explicit model texts.
- Content-Based Learning: Use subjects of interest to the students, integrating language learning with academic or personal interests.
- Explicitly teaching: Use detailed and explicit instructions to deconstruct language features and vocabulary.
- Provide multiple opportunities: Help students recycle language through topic based text types, sight words and known texts such as emails, text messages, brochures, etc.

Genres and some Australian Curriculum links for this level:

Genre	Topic	Australian Curriculum link
Comparative Report	Comparing English and Arabic	using modelled research skills and strategies to find information. (ACEEA136)
	Comparing Mammals and Reptiles	using simple comparative language, and reference items such as referential and demonstrative pronouns (ACEEA146)
Sequential Explanation	Lifecycle of Sunflowers	using known vocabulary and familiar text structures to find information (ACEEA135)
	Water Cycle	identifying the way information in texts has been ordered and structured (ACEEA137)
Argument	Is homework necessary?	collaborating to produce short texts that present facts, a point of view or opinion (ACEEA128)
	Mobile phones should be allowed in schools	identifying the persuasive nature of simple text types (ACEEA141)

Part Two – Post Beginner Level/Emerging – Comparative Report
Genre 1, Text 1
Teacher's Notes: What is a Comparative Report?

A comparative report analyses and compares information, or findings from multiple sources such as reference books, online searches, and classroom learning. The purpose of a comparative report is to highlight similarities and differences between the subjects being compared. These reports are commonly used in health and science subjects to report findings of experiments or researches.

When writing a comparative report, it is important to organise the information in a logical and coherent way, using headings, subheadings, images, and transitions to guide the reader through the report. Comparative reports provide EAL/D students opportunities to learn how to use compare and contrast language features more accurately. Comparative reports usually end with a conclusion.

For English as an Additional Language/Dialect (EAL/D) students, comparative reports can be a valuable tool for developing observation and analytical skills, as well as for communicating scientific or technical information in a clear and accessible way. They are an effective way to allow objective observations and build academic writing skills.

Features of a Comparative Report

- Sensory details – describing what we can see, hear, smell, taste, and feel.
- Clearly and logically organised – may include heading, sub-headings, images with captions, conclusion etc.
- Objective language – more facts, less personal opinions.
- Language features – adjectives and adverbs to create more depth.
- Compare and contrast vocabulary.

Text 1 – Comparative Report – English vs Home Language
English vs Arabic

Comparing their home languages to English can help EAL/D students understand the similarities and differences that are present in both languages. This will further support their learning and may help them overcome the hurdles of learning a new language. Writing simple comparative reports at the post-beginner level allows students to experiment with fundamental skills for academic and non-fiction work.

Genre 1 – Comparative Report
Comparing English and Arabic

Word Bank

communicate	<ul><li>talk with each other</li><li>ask or answer questions</li></ul>
Official language	<ul><li>The language used by the government of a country</li><li>The language taught in the schools of a country</li></ul>
vowels	a, e, i, o, u
On the other hand	We start a new sentence with this when we want to show that our new sentence has a different fact.
Word order	The way we write a sentence
however	We can use this instead of but – it shows that what we are writing is opposite or different from the sentence before.
confuse	Not really understanding something
similarities	What is the same?

Model Text – Annotated for whole class discussion

Comparing English and Arabic (Title – tells us what we are comparing)

Introduction (Sub-heading or Paragraph Title – tells us what the paragraph is about) All of us need languages to **communicate** with each other. Around the world, people speak many different languages. Many of these languages do not use the same letters as English. Sometimes, this makes it difficult for people to understand each other. In this report, we are going to compare English and Arabic and look at the different letters, sounds, and sentences of these languages. English is spoken in many countries of the world and Arabic is the official language of twenty-two countries.	• The first two or three sentences introduce the reader to the topic. • The last two sentences of the introduction tell the reader what this comparative report is about. • This word tells us that we are comparing two things.
English and Arabic letters (Sub-heading or Paragraph Title – tells us what the paragraph is about) In English, there are 26 letters but Arabic has 28 letters. Each letter in English has a special sound and sometimes one letter has many different sounds. For example, there are only five **vowels** in English but each vowel has more than one sound. On the other hand, Arabic only has six vowel sounds. They are the long and short sounds for a, i, and u. In Arabic, they also make a sound at the back of their throats, but we do not do this in English.	• Words and phrases that help us compare two things.
English and Arabic sentences (Sub-heading or Paragraph Title – tells us what the paragraph is about) Sentences in English and Arabic have different word order. For example, in English, we say, "I ate an apple". However, in Arabic we would say, "Ate I apple". We say the action first in Arabic but in English we say the person first. So, when Arabic or English speakers say something in the other language, it can sound wrong. Another important fact is that we write from the left to right in English but Arabic is written from right to left. This can also confuse Arabic speakers when they need to read in English.	• Words and phrases that help us compare two things.
Conclusion (Sub-heading or Paragraph Title – tells us what the paragraph is about) In conclusion, we can see that there are many important differences between English and Arabic although both languages are used for in many parts of the world. It is good for us to know them so we can help each other to understand and communicate more easily.	• Words and phrases that help us compare two things.

Discussion questions:
1. What are we writing?
2. What does the title tell us? Do you think it is important to have a title/ Why?
3. How do sub-headings help us?
4. How do the examples help?
5. Do you think it is important for us to talk about our home languages? Why?

Model Text – Non-Annotated

Comparing English and Arabic

Introduction

All of us need languages to communicate with each other. Around the world, people speak many different languages. Many of these languages do not use the same letters as English. Sometimes, this makes it difficult for people to understand each other. In this report, we are going to compare English and Arabic and look at the different letters, sounds, and sentences of these languages. English is spoken in many countries of the world whereas Arabic is the official language of twenty-two countries.

English and Arabic letters

In English, there are 26 letters but Arabic has 28 letters. Each letter in English has a special sound and sometimes one letter has many different sounds. For example, there are only five vowels in English but each vowel has more than one sound. On the other hand, Arabic only has six vowel sounds. They are the long and short sounds for a, i, and u. In Arabic, they also make a sound at the back of their throats, but we do not do this in English.

English and Arabic sentences

Sentences in English and Arabic have different word order. For example, in English, we say, "I ate an apple". However, in Arabic we would say, "Ate I apple". We say the action first in Arabic but in English we say the person first. So, when Arabic or English speakers say something in the other language, it can sound wrong. Another important fact is that we write from the left to right in English but Arabic is written from right to left. This can also confuse Arabic speakers when they need to read in English.

Conclusion

In conclusion, we can see that there are many important differences between English and Arabic although both languages are used for in many parts of the world. It is good for us to know them so we can help each other to understand and communicate more easily.

Reading and Viewing Activities

A: Word Level

1. List all the verbs you can see.

   [   ]

2. The verbs are written in the _____ tense because _____ .
3. List all the nouns you can see.

   [   ]

4. The nouns tell us that the writer is writing about _____
5. List all the compare and contrast words.

   [   ]

6. We use compare and contrast words when we want to show _____

B: Sentence Level

Answer the questions using complete sentences.

1. Why do we need languages?
   _____
2. What is this report comparing?
   _____
3. List three examples of how Arabic is different from English.
   a. _____
   b. _____
   c. _____
4. List two things that may confuse an Arabic speaker when they are writing in English.
   a. _____
   b. _____
5. Why do you think we need to know about different languages?
   _____
6. Do you or your family speak another language at home? _____
   a. What is it? _____
   b. Give one example of how it is different from English
   _____

Complete the information needed in the table below.

Title:	What does the title tell you?	
Introduction	Begins with: All of us need languages to communicate with each other. a. Do you think this is a good sentence to begin the paragraph? Why? b. How does this sentence show you that this is the introduction?	a. b.

Unlocking Genre 54

English and Arabic letters	a. Write the first sentence.	a.
	b. How does the first sentence link to the heading of this paragraph?	b.
	c. What other information does this paragraph have?	c.
	d. Is everything in this paragraph about English and Arabic letters? Why?	d.
English and Arabic sentences	a. How does the writer begin this paragraph?	a.
	b. Why do you think the writer started the paragraph with this sentence?	b.
	c. Create a sentence of your own that we could use to start this paragraph.	c.
Conclusion	a. What other way do you think we could start the first sentence in this paragraph?	a.
	b. How does the last sentence help the writer end this report?	b.

C: Text Level

Write TWO sentences to show what each paragraph is about. Then answer the two questions.

Paragraph 1	
Paragraph 2	
Paragraph 3	
Paragraph 4	
Think about how the writer has written about different things in each paragraph. a. How are the paragraphs connecting to each other? b. How will you use this idea in your own writing?	a. b.

Unlocking Genre 55

Functional Grammar

	Describe	What?	Extra Information
many	interesting	languages	In the world.
		people	
		letters	
		report	
		sounds	
		sentences	

D: Writing

Talk to your family to find out more about your home language. Write a comparative report about your home language and English. Use the questions in the table below to help you.

Title:	Comparing English and _____
Introduction	a. Why do we need languages? b. Where do people use this language? c. What are going to do in this report?
English and _____ letters	a. How many letters? b. Are they written the same way as in English? c. Are there any different sounds? Give one example.
English and _____ sentences	a. Are there any similarities? b. Are there any differences? Give one example. c. Do they write from left to right or the other way around? How does this make you feel?
Conclusion	a. Differences and similarities. b. How does this help/not help you? c. Why do we need to compare our home language with English?

Part Two – Post Beginner Level – Comparative Report

Genre 1, Text 2

Teacher's Notes: What is a Comparative Report?

A comparative report analyses and compares information, or findings from multiple sources such as reference books, online searches, and classroom learning. The purpose of a comparative report is to highlight similarities and differences between the subjects being compared. These reports are commonly used in health and science subjects to report findings of experiments or researches.

When writing a comparative report, it is important to organise the information in a logical and coherent way, using headings, subheadings, images, and transitions to guide the reader through the report. Comparative reports provide EAL/D students opportunities to learn how to use compare and contrast language features more accurately. Comparative reports usually end with a conclusion.

For English as an Additional Language/Dialect (EAL/D) students, comparative reports can be a valuable tool for developing observation and analytical skills, as well as for communicating scientific or technical information in a clear and accessible way. They are an effective way to allow objective observations and build academic writing skills.

Features of a Comparative Report

- Sensory details – describing what we can see, hear, smell, taste, and feel.
- Clearly and logically organised – may include heading, sub-headings, images with captions, conclusion etc.
- Objective language – more facts, less personal opinions.
- Language features – adjectives and adverbs to create more depth.
- Compare and contrast vocabulary.

Text 2 – Comparative Report

Mammals vs Reptiles

Comparing two different animal species can help EAL/D students understand the similarities and differences that are present in the animal world. This will help set them up for future scientific exploration and is an example of how we can teach English using cross-curricular subject areas. Writing simple comparative reports at the post-beginner level allows students to experiment with fundamental skills for academic and non-fiction work.

Genre 1 – Comparative Report
Comparing Mammals and Reptiles

Word Bank

similarities	What is the same in both types of animals.
differences	What is different in both types of animals.
body temperature	Tells us how warm or cold the body is.
features	• What do they look like. • What do they have on their bodies.
predators	Animals that hunt and eat other animals.
prevent	stop
usually	Most of the time
hatch	Eggs break and the babies come out

Mammals   Reptiles

Unlocking Genre

Model Text – Annotated for whole class discussion

Comparing Mammals and Reptiles (Title – tells us what we are comparing)

Introduction (Sub-heading or Paragraph Title – tells us what the paragraph is about) There are many types of animals in the world such as mammals, reptiles, insects, fishes, birds, and many more. They may all have some similarities and differences. Some animals live only on land and some live in water. However, there are animals that can live in both land and water. In this report, we will be comparing mammals and reptiles. We can keep some mammals such as cats, dogs, and rabbits as pets. Some people also keep reptiles such as lizards, snakes, and turtles as pets.	• The first two or three sentences introduce the reader to the topic. • The last two sentences of the introduction tell the reader what this comparative report is about. • This word tells us that we are comparing two things.
What are they? (Sub-heading or Paragraph Title – tells us what the paragraph is about) Mammals are warm blooded animals because their body temperature stays the same even when the outside temperature is very hot or very cold. On the other hand, reptiles are cold-blooded animals because their bodies need outside temperature to keep them warm. There are mammals and reptiles that live on land and water. However, the mammals that live in water cannot live on land but some reptiles can live in both land and water. Some examples of mammals are lions, elephants, cows, whales, kangaroos, and dogs. Crocodiles, lizards, and turtles are examples of reptiles. The biggest animal in the world is the blue whale, which is a mammal. Human beings are also mammals.	• Words and phrases that help us compare two things.
Features (Sub-heading or Paragraph Title – tells us what the paragraph is about) Mammals have hair or fur on their skin. This helps to protect their bodies and keep them warm when it is cold outside. On the other hand, reptiles have scales on their skin. The scales help to keep reptiles save from predators and prevent their skins from becoming too dry. However, both mammals and reptiles breathe using their lungs.	• Words and phrases that help us compare two things.

While both mammals and reptiles have teeth that help them eat, they are different from each other. Mammals have a few types of teeth in their mouths which can help them to eat whatever they choose. Some mammals are herbivores, so they only eat plants, while other mammals are carnivores and they eat only meat. However, although some reptiles are carnivores and some are herbivores, they usually have only one type of teeth in their mouths depending on what they eat.  Mammals and reptile have many different features.	
Babies (Sub-heading or Paragraph Title – tells us what the paragraph is about) Mammals give birth to their babies and feed them milk from the mothers' bodies. They take care of their babies when they are young. In contrast, reptiles lay eggs and leave the eggs to hatch on their own. They usually do not take care of their babies.	• Words and phrases that help us compare two things.
Conclusion (Sub-heading or Paragraph Title – tells us what the paragraph is about) Although both mammals and reptiles have some similarities such as lungs to breathe and living in land or water, there are many differences between them. For example, mammals give birth to live babies and care for them, but reptiles lay eggs and leave them to hatch on their own. We can find both mammals and reptiles on land and in water. It is important for us to understand that all animals have many interesting features and different eating styles.	• Words and phrases that help us compare two things.

Discussion questions:
1. Look at the first sentence in the first paragraph? Do you think this is a good way to start this report? Why?
2. What does the title tell us? Do you think it is important to have a title/ Why?
3. How do sub-headings help us?
4. Look at the part titles 'Features". How many paragraphs are there in this part? Why do you think the writer has done this?
5. What do we do when we are writing a comparative report?
6. Look at the sentence below the picture. What do we call it? What does it do?

Model Text – Non-Annotated

Comparing Mammals and Reptiles

Introduction

There are many types of animals in the world such as mammals, reptiles, insects, fishes, birds, and many more. They may all have some similarities and differences. Some animals live only on land and some live in water. However, there are animals that can live in both land and water. In this report, we will be comparing mammals and reptiles. We can keep some mammals such as cats, dogs, and rabbits as pets. Some people also keep reptiles such as lizards, snakes, and turtles as pets.

What are they?

Mammals are warm blooded animals because their body temperature stays the same even when the outside temperature is very hot or very cold. On the other hand, reptiles are cold-blooded animals because their bodies need outside temperature to keep them warm. There are mammals and reptiles that live on land and water. However, the mammals that live in water cannot live on land but some reptiles can live in both land and water. Some examples of mammals are lions, elephants, cows, whales, kangaroos, and dogs. Crocodiles, lizards, and turtles are examples of reptiles. The biggest animal in the world is the blue whale, which is a mammal. Human beings are also mammals.

Features

Mammals have hair or fur on their skin. This helps to protect their bodies and keep them warm when it is cold outside. On the other hand, reptiles have scales on their skin. The scales help to keep reptiles save from predators and prevent their skins from becoming too dry. However, both mammals and reptiles breathe using their lungs.

While both mammals and reptiles have teeth that help them eat, they are different from each other. Mammals have a few types of teeth in their mouths which can help them to eat whatever they choose. Some mammals are herbivores, so they only eat plants, while other mammals are carnivores and they eat only meat. However, although some reptiles are carnivores and some are herbivores, they usually have only one type of teeth in their mouths depending on what they eat.

Mammals and reptile have many different features.

Babies

Mammals give birth to their babies and feed them milk from the mothers' bodies. They take care of their babies when they are young. In contrast, reptiles lay eggs and leave the eggs to hatch on their own. They usually do not take care of their babies.

Conclusion

Although both mammals and reptiles have some similarities such as lungs to breathe and living in land or water, there are many differences between them. For example, mammals give birth to live babies and care for them, but reptiles lay eggs and leave them to hatch on their own. We can find both mammals and reptiles on land and in water. It is interesting to know that all animals have many interesting features and different eating styles.

Reading and Viewing Activities

A: Word Level

1. List all the verbs you can see.

2. The verbs are written in the _____ tense because _____.
3. List all the nouns you can see.

4. The nouns tell us that the writer is writing about _____
5. List all the pronouns you can see.

6. What do we use pronouns for? _____
7. List all the compare and contrast words.

8. We use compare and contrast words when we want to show _____

B: Sentence Level

Answer the questions using complete sentences.

1. Why do we need an introduction?
   _____
2. What is this report comparing?
   _____
3. List three examples of how mammals are different from reptiles.
   a. _____
   b. _____
   c. _____
4. List two things that are similar in both mammals and reptiles.
   a. _____
   b. _____
5. What is an interesting comparison of body temperature of mammals and reptiles?
   _____
6. Look at the caption below the picture. Write one new caption using your own words. Give a reason for your caption.
   a. My new caption _____
   b. My reason for writing this caption _____

Complete the information needed in the table below.

Title:	What does the title tell you?	
Introduction	Begins with: There are many types of animals in the world such as mammals, reptiles, insects... a. Do you think this is a good sentence to begin the paragraph? Why? b. How does this sentence show you that this is the introduction?	a. b.
What are they?	a. Write your own sub-heading b. Link the first and second sentences using 'and'. You can leave out some words. c. What does the last sentence tell you?	a. b. c.
Features	a. Write your own sub-heading. b. What is the first feature the writer is comparing? c. Create a sentence of your own that we could use to start this paragraph.	a. b. c.
Babies	a. How does the writer compare mammals and reptiles in this paragraph?	a.
Conclusion	a. What other way do you think we could start the first sentence in this paragraph? b. How does the last sentence help the writer end this report?	a. b.

Unlocking Genre 63

C: Text Level

Write TWO sentences to show what each paragraph is about. Then answer the two questions.

Paragraph 1	
Paragraph 2	
Paragraph 3	
Paragraph 4	
Think about how the writer has written about different things in each paragraph. a. How are the paragraphs connecting to each other? b. How will you use this idea in your own writing?	a. b.

Functional Grammar

	Describe	What?	Extra Information
many	interesting	animals	in the world.
		land	
		temperature	
		fur	
		scales	
		teeth	

D: Writing

Think about TWO animals. Write a comparative report about them. Use the questions in the table below to help you.

Title:	Comparing _____ and _____
Introduction	a. How many types of animals are there in the world? b. Where do these animals live? c. What are going to do in this report?
Your own sub-heading/title	a. Body temperature. b. Do they live on land or in water? c. Some other examples.
Your own sub-heading/title	a. Discuss hair/fur/skin, teeth, food. b. Are there any similarities? Give one example c. Are there any differences? Give one example.
Your own sub-heading/title	a. How do they have babies? b. Differences and similarities between the two animals you have chosen.
Conclusion	a. General similarities and differences in both. b. Good sentence to end.

Part Two – Post Beginner Level – Sequential Explanation

Genre 2, Text 1

Teacher's Notes: What is a Sequential Explanation?

A sequential explanation explains a process or series of steps in a logical order. The purpose of a sequential explanation is to provide clear instructions that can be followed to achieve a specific outcome or complete a task.

Sequential explanations can be found in many types of documents, including user guides, manuals, tutorials, or technical writing. They may also include an introduction that outlines the purpose of the explanation, a list of materials or equipment needed, and a step-by-step description of the process.

When teaching how to write a sequential explanation to English as an Additional Language/Dialect (EAL/D) students, it is important to explicitly discuss:

- How students can use clear and precise language to break the sequence into small, manageable steps.
- The use of appropriate sequencing words and phrases, such as first, next, then, and finally, to help the reader follow the sequence in a logical order.
- Adding visual aids such as diagrams, illustrations, picture sequences etc.

For EAL/D students, sequential explanations can be a valuable tool for developing observation and analytical skills of natural cycles. They also help EAL/D students to write about scientific or technical information in a clear sequence. They are an effective way to allow objective observations and build academic writing skills.

Features of a Sequential Explanation

- Sensory details – describing what we can see, hear, smell, taste, and feel.
- Clearly and logically organised – may include cyclic images, headings, sub-headings, images with captions, conclusion etc.
- Objective language – more facts, less personal opinions.
- Language features – adjectives and adverbs to create more depth.
- Use of appropriate sequencing vocabulary.

Text 1 – Sequential Explanation

Lifecyle of Sunflowers

Writing sequential explanations can help EAL/D students explore the concepts of chronological timelines and natural cycles found in nature. They lay the foundations for writing scientific and historical reports. Writing simple sequential explanations at the post-beginner level allows students to experiment with fundamental skills for academic and non-fiction work.

Genre 2 – Sequential Explanation
Lifecycle of Sunflowers

Word Bank

species	types
lifecycle	growing from seeds to adult plants
soil	Earth and sand where we plant seeds
nutrition	food

Picture of Lifecycle of a Sunflower (example below)

Labelled parts of a sunflower (example)

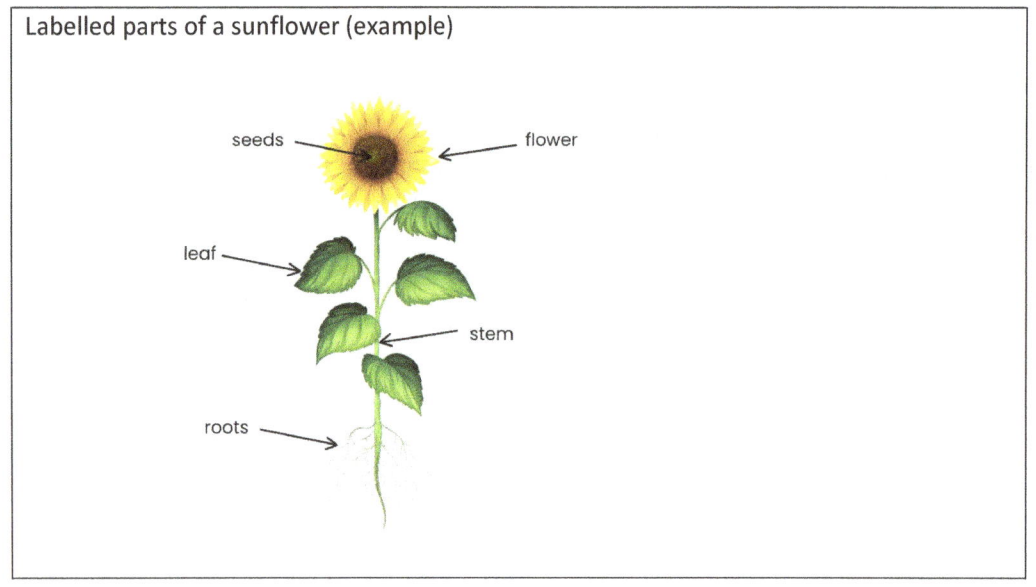

Model Text – Annotated for whole class discussion

Lifecyle of Sunflowers **(Title – tells us what our sequential explanation is about)**

Introduction **(Sub-heading or Paragraph Title – tells us what the paragraph is about)** There are many types of plants in the world. Some plants have flowers. They are called flowering plants. Sunflowers are a type of flowering plants. There are around sixty species of sunflowers. Sunflowers have a lifecycle that begins as seeds. In this sequential explanation, we will look more closely at the lifecycle of sunflowers.	• The first two or three sentences introduce the reader to the topic. • The last sentence of the introduction tells the reader what this sequential explanation is about.
The first stage (Sub-heading or Paragraph Title – tells us what the paragraph is about) Firstly, we plant the sunflower seeds in good soil that is in a warm, sunny place. We need to water the seeds often until they germinate into seedlings after one to two weeks.	• Words and phrases that help us write in a correct sequence.
The second stage (Sub-heading or Paragraph Title – tells us what the paragraph is about) Next, the seedlings start to grow. They have tiny roots that go down into the soil to look for water and nutrition. A green stem will start to grow out of the soil. The stem helps the seedling grow more strongly.	• Words and phrases that help us write in a correct sequence.
The third stage (Sub-heading or Paragraph Title – tells us what the paragraph is about) After a few weeks, the seedling will become a baby sunflower plant. It will start sprouting a few more leaves that grow upward to find the sun. The leaves use sunlight, water, and carbon dioxide to make more food for the plant. This process is called photosynthesis	• Words and phrases that help us write in a correct sequence.
The fourth stage (Sub-heading or Paragraph Title – tells us what the paragraph is about) Then, the sunflower plant grows taller and stronger. A bud grows out of the stem. The bud will slowly continue to open and become a fully bloomed flower about three months.	• Words and phrases that help us write in a correct sequence.
The fifth stage (Sub-heading or Paragraph Title – tells us what the paragraph is about) Finally, the sunflower starts to dry and die. When the flower dies, it will drop its seeds. We can use these seeds to start the lifecycle of the sunflower all over again.	• Words and phrases that help us write in a correct sequence.

Discussion questions:
1. What are we writing?
2. What is a sequential explanation? Is it fiction or non-fiction?
3. What does the title tell us? Do you think it is important to have a title/ Why?
4. How do sub-headings help us?
5. What are the words we use to help us write in the correct sequence?
6. Can you see the other words in the sub-headings that also show sequence?

Model Text – Non-Annotated

Lifecycle of Sunflowers

Introduction

There are many types of plants in the world. Some plants have flowers. They are called flowering plants. Sunflowers are a type of flowering plants. There are around sixty species of sunflowers. Sunflowers have a lifecycle that begins as seeds. In this sequential explanation, we will look more closely at the lifecycle of sunflowers.

The first stage

Firstly, we plant the sunflower seeds in good soil that is in a warm, sunny place. We need to water the seeds often until they germinate into seedlings after one to two weeks.

The second stage

Next, the seedlings start to grow. They have tiny roots that go down into the soil to look for water and nutrition. A green stem will start to grow out of the soil. The stem helps the seedling grow more strongly.

The third stage

After a few weeks, the seedling will become a baby sunflower plant. It will start sprouting a few more leaves that grow upward to find the sun. The leaves use sunlight, water, and carbon dioxide to make more food for the plant. This process is called photosynthesis

The fourth stage

Then, the sunflower plant grows taller and stronger. A bud grows out of the stem. The bud will slowly continue to open and become a fully bloomed flower about three months.

The fifth stage

Finally, the sunflower starts to dry and die. When the flower dies, it will drop its seeds. We can use these seeds to start the lifecycle of the sunflower all over again

Reading and Viewing Activities

A: Word Level

1. List all the verbs you can see.

2. The verbs are written in the _____ tense because _____.
3. List all the nouns you can see.

4. The nouns tell us that the writer is writing about _____
5. List all the sequence words.

6. We use sequence words when we want to show _____

B: Sentence Level

Answer the questions using complete sentences.

1. What do sunflowers begin life as?
   _____
2. What is this sequential explanation telling us?
   _____
3. List the first three stages of the lifecycle of a sunflower.
4. _____
5. _____
6. _____
7. What finally happens?
   _____
8. How does the lifecycle of a sunflower continue?
   _____

Complete the sentences below. Then rearrange them in the correct sequence by writing numbers 1 – 6.

Then,	
Firstly,	
There are	
Finally,	
After a few weeks,	
Next,	

C: Text Level

Write TWO sentences to show what each paragraph is about. Then answer the two questions.

Paragraph 1	
Paragraph 2	
Paragraph 3	
Paragraph 4	
Paragraph 5	
Paragraph 6	

Think about how the writer has written about different things in each paragraph. 1. How are the paragraphs connecting to each other? 2. How will you use this idea in your own writing?	a. b.

Functional Grammar

	Describe	What?	Extra Information
many	types of	sunflowers	in the world.
		plants	
		seeds	
		soil	
		leaves	
		seedling	

D: Writing

Look at the picture below and write a sequential explanation about the lifecycle of a bean plant. Use words from the Lifecycle of Sunflowers to help you.

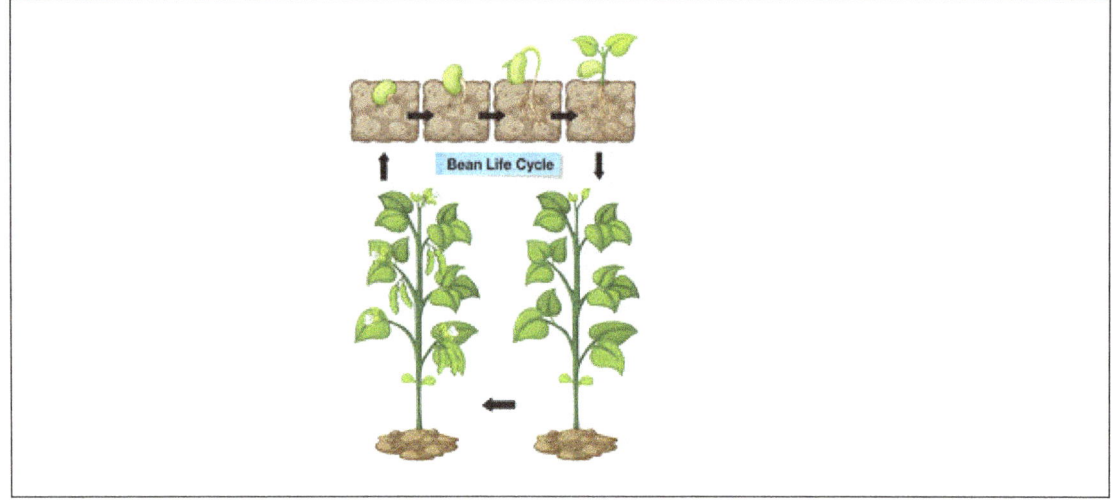

Unlocking Genre   70

Part Two – Post Beginner Level – Sequential Explanation
Genre 2, Text 2
Teacher's Notes: What is a Sequential Explanation?

A sequential explanation explains a process or series of steps in a logical order. Another purpose of a sequential explanation is to provide clear explanations about natural phenomenon that can support understanding of a specific process.

Sequential explanations can be found in many types of documents, including user guides, manuals, tutorials, or technical writing. They may also include an introduction that outlines the purpose of the explanation, a list of materials or equipment needed, and a step-by-step description of the process.

When teaching how to write a sequential explanation to English as an Additional Language/Dialect (EAL/D) students, it is important to explicitly discuss:

- How students can use clear and precise language to break the sequence into small, manageable steps.
- The use of appropriate sequencing words and phrases, such as first, next, then, and finally, to help the reader follow the sequence in a logical order.
- Adding visual aids such as diagrams, illustrations, picture sequences etc.

For EAL/D students, sequential explanations can be a valuable tool for developing observation and analytical skills of natural cycles. They also help EAL/D students to write about scientific or technical information in a clear sequence. They are an effective way to allow objective observations and build academic writing skills.

Features of a Sequential Explanation

- Sensory details – describing what we can see, hear, smell, taste, and feel.
- Clearly and logically organised – may include cyclic images, headings, sub-headings, images with captions, conclusion etc.
- Objective language – more facts, less personal opinions.
- Language features – adjectives and adverbs to create more depth.
- Use of appropriate sequencing vocabulary.

Text 2 – Sequential Explanation
Water Cycle

Writing sequential explanations can help EAL/D students explore the concepts of chronological timelines and natural cycles found in nature. They lay the foundations for writing scientific and historical reports. Writing simple sequential explanations at the post-beginner level allows students to experiment with fundamental skills for academic and non-fiction work.

Genre 2 – Sequential Explanation
Water Cycle

Word Bank

stages	steps
evaporation	when water gets hot and goes up as steam or gas
condensation	when water cools down like when we pour iced water in a glass and we can touch and feel that the outside of the glass is cold and wet
liquid	water, coffee, tea, milk, juice etc.
precipitation	happens when there is too much water in the clouds and it rains or snows.
consequently	something that makes another thing happen
hail	ice rain
collection	where rain water is collected in rivers, lakes, oceans…

Picture of Water Cycle

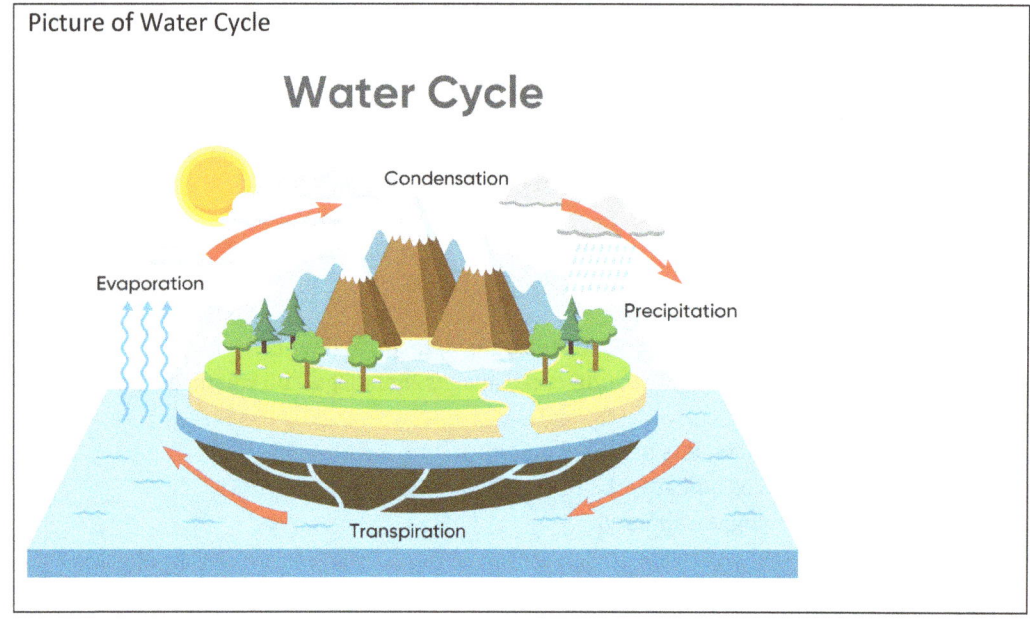

Model Text – Annotated for whole class discussion

Water Cycle (Title – tells us what our sequential explanation is about)

Introduction **(Sub-heading or Paragraph Title – tells us what the paragraph is about)** All living things need water. Animals use water for drinking or cooling their bodies. Humans use water for more things such as drinking, cooking, cleaning, and washing. Without water, living things will die. Do you know how water comes down from the sky when it rains? In order for us to have water, we need to have a good water cycle. There are four important stages in a water cycle; evaporation, condensation, precipitation, and collection. During this cycle, water changes into solid, liquid, and gas. In this sequential explanation, we will look at what happens during these stages.	• The first two or three sentences introduce the reader to the topic. • Thinking question for the readers so they feel interested to continue reading. • The last sentence of the introduction tells the reader what this sequential explanation is about.
Evaporation (Sub-heading or Paragraph Title – tells us what the paragraph is about)  This is the first stage of the water cycle. When water in rivers, lakes, and oceans get hot from the sun's heat, it changes into steam. Think of what happens when we boil water. We can see the steam rising up. In the same way, the steam from rivers, lakes, and oceans rises up into the air. During this stage, water changes into gas.	• Words and phrases that help us write in a correct sequence.
Condensation (Sub-heading or Paragraph Title – tells us what the paragraph is about)  The next stage is condensation. As the steam rises, it loses its heat and cools down. During this process called condensation, it becomes liquid and creates clouds. We can see an example of this when we pour very cold water into a glass on a hot day. Condensation happens on the outside of the glass because the warm air outside the glass changes to liquid when it touches the cold glass.	• Words and phrases that help us write in a correct sequence.

Precipitation (Sub-heading or Paragraph Title – tells us what the paragraph is about)	• Words and phrases that help us write in a correct sequence.
 **Consequently**, when we see dark clouds, it means that enough water has condensed and the clouds are getting heavy with liquid. **When** enough condensation has taken place, precipitation happens. This can happen in the form of liquid rain, or solid snow and hail.	
Collection (Sub-heading or Paragraph Title – tells us what the paragraph is about)	• Words and phrases that help us write in a correct sequence.
 **The final stage** is collection. This is when the evaporated water falls down to earth as precipitation. The water then returns to the rivers, lakes, and oceans. It also returns as snow during cold winters and on top of very high mountains. The cycle starts all over again.	

Discussion questions:
1. What are we writing?
2. What is a sequential explanation? Is it fiction or non-fiction?
3. What does the title tell us? Do you think it is important to have a title/ Why?
4. How do sub-headings help us?
5. What are the words we use to help us write in the correct sequence? How do these words help us understand what happens first, next, then, and finally?

Model Text – Non-Annotated

Water Cycle
Introduction

All living things need water. Animals use water for drinking or cooling their bodies. Humans use water for more things such as drinking, cooking, cleaning, and washing. Without water, living things will die. Do you know how water comes down from the sky when it rains?

In order for us to have water, we need to have a good water cycle. There are four important stages in a water cycle; evaporation, condensation, precipitation, and collection. During this cycle, water changes into solid, liquid, and gas. In this sequential explanation, we will look at what happens during these stages.

Evaporation

 This is the first stage of the water cycle. When water in rivers, lakes, and oceans get hot from the sun's heat, it changes into steam. Think of what happens when we boil water. We can see the steam rising up. In the same way, the steam from rivers, lakes, and oceans rises up into the air. During this stage, water changes into gas.

Condensation

The next stage is condensation. As the steam rises, it loses its heat and cools down. During this process called condensation, it becomes liquid and creates clouds. We can see an example of this when we pour very cold water into a glass on a hot day. Condensation happens on the outside of the glass because the warm air outside the glass changes to liquid when it touches the cold glass.

Precipitation

Consequently, when we see dark clouds, it means that enough water has condensed and the clouds are getting heavy with liquid. When enough condensation has taken place, precipitation happens. This can happen in the form of liquid rain, or solid snow and hail.

Collection

The final stage is collection. This is when the evaporated water falls down to earth as precipitation. The water then returns to the rivers, lakes, and oceans. It also returns as snow during cold winters and on top of very high mountains. The cycle starts all over again.

Reading and Viewing Activities

A: Word Level

1. List all the verbs you can see.
2. The verbs are written in the _____ tense because _____.
3. List all the nouns you can see.
4. The nouns tell us that the writer is writing about _____
5. List all the sequence words.
6. We use sequence words when we want to show _____
7. List the four stages of the water cycle in the correct order:
   a. _____
   b. _____
   c. _____
   d. _____

B: Sentence Level

Answer the questions using complete sentences.

1. Why do you think water is important for living things?
2. What is this sequential explanation telling us?

Unlocking Genre   75

3. List and explain what happens to water during the four stages of the water cycle.

Complete the sentences below. Add another sentence of your own to each stage. Then write numbers 1-5 to correctly order the stages.

The final stage	
The next stage	
All living things	
Consequently	
This is the first stage	

C: Text Level

Write TWO sentences to explain what each paragraph is about. Then answer the two questions.

Paragraph 1	
Paragraph 2	
Paragraph 3	
Paragraph 4	
Paragraph 5	
Think about how the writer has written about different things in each paragraph. 1. How are the paragraphs connecting to each other? 2. How will you use this idea to plan your own writing?	a. b.

Functional Grammar

	Describe	What?	Extra Information
a	wild	animal	needs drinking water.
		water	
		rivers	
		snow	
		clouds	
		mountains	

D: Writing

Draw a picture of the water cycle. Label each stage. Write two sentences of your own to explain each stage.

Part Two – Post Beginner Level – Argument

Genre 3, Text 1

Teacher's Notes: What is an Argument?

An argument is a type of writing that presents a position or viewpoint on a particular issue or topic, and provides evidence and reasoning to support that position. The purpose of an argument is to persuade the reader to understand, accept, and support the writer's point of view. Sometimes arguments may convince the reader to take a specific course of action.

There are many forms of arguments including essays, speeches, debates, and editorials. Arguments should have a clear structure so they are easy for readers to follow. The structure of an argument should include:

- Introduction – this outlines the topic, provides background information, and a summary of the evidence that may be presented.
- The thesis statement – one statement of the main argument.
- Body paragraphs – two to three paragraphs that provide:
    - examples
    - statistics
    - research
    - anecdotal and expert opinions
    - provide rebuttal to counter arguments that may arise
- Conclusion – restates the thesis and summarises the arguments.

When teaching how to write arguments to English as an Additional Language/Dialect (EAL/D) students, it is important to explicitly discuss:

- The use of persuasive language.
- How to do simple research to find statistics and expert opinions.
- Adding visual aids such as graphs, diagrams, illustrations, etc.

For EAL/D students, writing arguments can be a valuable tool for developing critical thinking, analysing simple data, and improving their communication skills. They also help EAL/D students to demonstrate how they can support their views with factual and anecdotal evidence. Arguments are an effective way to present objective observations and build academic writing skills.

Features of an Argument

- Clear and focused thesis statement/question.
- Clearly and logically organised – each fact, data, expert opinion should support the thesis statement.
- Evidence – statistics, expert opinion, examples, etc.
- Language features – persuasive language to convince the reader.
- Tone – objective and avoid personal attacks.
- Conclusion – summary of main points that support the thesis statement/question.

Text 1 – Argument

Mobile phone should be allowed in schools

Writing arguments can help EAL/D students explore the concepts of providing supporting evidence to strengthen their points of view. They lay the foundations for writing and other communication skills such as debates, oral presentations, and exploring social and political issues. Writing simple arguments at the post-beginner level allows students to experiment with fundamental skills for academic writing, presenting speeches, and other non-fiction reports.

Genre 3 – Argument
Mobile phones should be allowed in schools

Word Bank

currently	At the moment
fears	Something we are afraid of
distracted	Not paying attention
psychologist	Someone who helps us take care of our thoughts and feelings
investment	Doing this will have good outcomes
conducted	Completed
impact	Change than can happen when we do something
negative feedback	Comments that can make us feel sad and upset
propose	Suggest
awareness	Knowing and understanding something
revisit	Look again
socialise	Talk and share
hurtful	Words that can make us very upset or hurt our feelings
self-control	Stopping ourselves from doing bad things even when we are angry
effectively	Correctly
band aid	Small plaster to cover cuts

Model Text – Annotated for whole class discussion

Mobile phones should be allowed in schools **(Title – tells us what our argument is about)**

Introduction **(Sub-heading or Paragraph Title – tells us what the paragraph is about)**	• Thesis statement of the argument. • The first two or three sentences introduce the reader to the topic. • Expert opinion. • Counter arguments/persuasive language • The last sentence of the introduction tells the reader what this argument will do.
In this argument, we are going to look at why "Mobile phones should be allowed in schools". Currently, many countries have banned the use of mobile phones in schools. In Australia, all states have now banned the use of mobile phones during school hours. The two main reasons provided by the governments are fears of cyberbullying and students performing badly due to being distracted during lessons. According to Dr Michael Carr-Gregg, a leading Australian psychologist, 'banning mobile phones in high schools from the first to bell to last would be an investment in students' mental health'. However, a one-year study conducted in Sweden in 2020 found that banning mobile phones did not have any impact on student performance. Also, we know that more students are bullied while they are in school. Cyber bullying often happens after school hours, when people leave negative feedback on social media platforms. Therefore, the argument about fear of cyber bullying is not strong enough for a total mobile phone ban in schools. Banning something has never really worked. It actually makes the problem more interesting and encourages students to find ways to beat the system. We will propose that the better way to deal with mobile phones is through education and awareness programmes, as we have done with many other social issues in the past.	
Student performance (Sub-heading or Paragraph Title – tells us what the paragraph is about)	• Topic sentence • Counter arguments/persuasive language • Statistics
One of the main reasons given for a total mobile phone ban at schools is that students are distracted and therefore their academic performance has dropped. Let us revisit the situation during the Covid lockdowns. During this time, students were expected to heavily rely on technology, including mobile phones to attend online lessons and socialise with their friends and family so they stay mentally positive. This counters the argument by Dr Carr-Gregg that mobile phones are a threat to students' mental health. In fact, most researches show that most of the student performance during Covid was affected by students not being able to complete practical parts of their subjects. This was mostly impacted by school closures rather than the use of mobile phones. Furthermore, in Australia, many students did extremely well in their year 12 exams despite being in lockdown and having continuous access to their mobile phones. According to The Age, the average Australian Tertiary Admission Rank (ATAR) score in 2021 was a high 87.1%. This proves that mobile phones do not actually have a negative impact on student performance.	

Unlocking Genre 80

Cyber Bullying (Sub-heading or Paragraph Title – tells us what the paragraph is about) The second reason given for total mobile phone bans in schools is the fear of cyber bullying. According to the E-Safety Commissioner of the Australian government, "cyber bullying is when someone uses the internet to be mean to a child or young person so they feel bad or upset". This includes "posts, comments, texts, messages, chats, livestreams, memes, images, videos, and emails". The key word here is "internet". As we all know, the internet is not only available in mobile phones. Cyber bullies will not stop simply because they cannot use their mobile phones during school. They can get onto their mobile phones as soon as school is over or go home and use their computers to leave hurtful remarks. While we are not supporting cyber bullying, the important thing to do is to educate students about the effects of this. Banning mobile phones is definitely not the answer. It is more effective to teach students how to use their mobile phones safely. When students behave badly or bully other students in schools, we do not ban them from coming to school. Instead, we talk to them or their parents and try to teach them how to behave better. It is the same with using mobile phones. Banning them takes away the opportunity to learn self-control and may actually contribute to more cyber bullying after school hours as we have not included parents and usage at home as important factors when we ban mobile phones in schools. We should be including parents and students in educational programmes about cyber safety and bullying instead of using a total ban as a band aid to a serious problem.	• Topic sentence • Expert opinion • Counter arguments/persuasive language
Conclusion (Sub-heading or Paragraph Title – tells us what the paragraph is about) In conclusion, it is a fact that we now live in a digital world. Our latest progress is the use of Artificial Intelligence (AI) for many things in our lives. Research by Internet Study Lab suggests that schools use technology for almost 95% of their work including collecting student data. So, students' personal information does not become private just because we ban mobile phones in schools. It is better to learn how to use technology safely rather than totally ban it. Therefore, we should be looking at ways where mobile phones can be used effectively during some lessons including educating our students on social skills and safety strategies. We need to trust our students and understand that in our world today, it is extremely difficult to get jobs if we do not have digital skills including using our mobile phones to connect with our organisation. This includes keeping their personal information safe and learning strategies to counter cyber bullying. Whether we like it or not, technology is here to stay. Instead of pretending that a mobile phone ban in schools will have a positive impact on students' learning and mental health, it is better to face reality and support students to become more effective mobile phone users.	• Topic sentence • Expert opinion • Counter arguments/persuasive language • Statistics

Discussion questions:
1. What are we writing?
2. What is an argument?
3. What does the title tell us? Do you think it is important to have a title/ Why?
4. How do sub-headings help us?
5. What are the words we use to help us persuade our readers? How do these words help us convey our message?

Model Text – Non-Annotated

Mobile phones should be allowed in schools

Introduction

In this argument, we are going to look at why "Mobile phones should be allowed in schools". Currently, many countries have banned the use of mobile phones in schools. In Australia, all states have now banned the use of mobile phones during school hours. The two main reasons provided by the governments are fears of cyberbullying and students performing badly due to being distracted during lessons. According to Dr Michael Carr-Gregg, a leading Australian psychologist, 'banning mobile phones in high schools from the first to bell to last would be an investment in students' mental health'.

However, a one-year study conducted in Sweden in 2020 found that banning mobile phones did not have any impact on student performance. Also, we know that more students are bullied while they are in school. Cyber bullying often happens after school hours, when people leave insulting feedback on social media platforms. Therefore, the argument about fear of cyber bullying is not strong enough for a total mobile phone ban in schools. Banning something has never really worked. It actually makes the problem more interesting and encourages students to find ways to beat the system. We will propose that the better way to deal with mobile phones is through education and awareness programmes, as we have done with many other social issues in the past.

Student performance

One of the main reasons given for a total mobile phone ban at schools is that students are distracted and therefore their academic performance has dropped. Let us revisit the situation during the Covid lockdowns. During this time, students were expected to heavily rely on technology, including mobile phones to attend online lessons and socialise with their friends and family so they stay mentally positive. This counters the argument by Dr Carr-Gregg that mobile phones are a threat to students' mental health.

In fact, most researches show that most of the student performance during Covid was affected by students not being able to complete practical parts of their subjects. This was mostly impacted by school closures rather than the use of mobile phones. Furthermore, in Australia, many students did extremely well in their year 12 exams despite being in lockdown and having continuous access to their mobile phones. According to The Age, the average Australian Tertiary Admission Rank (ATAR) score in 2021 was a high 87.1%. This proves that mobile phones do not actually have a negative impact on student performance.

Cyber Bullying

The second reason given for total mobile phone bans in schools is the fear of cyber bullying. According to the E-Safety Commissioner of the Australian government, "cyber bullying is when someone uses the internet to be mean to a child or young person so they feel bad or upset". This includes "posts, comments, texts, messages, chats, livestreams, memes, images, videos, and emails".

The key word here is "internet". As we all know, the internet is not only available in mobile phones. Cyber bullies will not stop simply because they cannot use their mobile phones during school. They can get onto their mobile phones as soon as school is over or go home and use their computers to leave hurtful remarks.

While we are not supporting cyber bullying, the important thing to do is to educate students about the effects of this. Banning mobile phones is definitely not the answer. It is more effective to teach students how to use their mobile phones safely. When students behave badly or bully other students in schools, we do not ban them from coming to school. Instead, we talk to them or their parents and try to teach them how to behave better. It is the same with using mobile phones. Banning them takes away the opportunity to learn self-control and may actually contribute to more cyber bullying after school hours as we have not included parents and usage at home as important factors when we ban mobile phones in schools. We should be including parents and students in educational programmes about cyber safety and bullying instead of using a total ban as a band aid to a serious problem.

Conclusion

In conclusion, it is a fact that we now live in a digital world. Our latest progress is the use of Artificial Intelligence (AI) in our everyday life. Research by Internet Study Lab suggests that schools use technology for almost 95% of their work including collecting student data. So, students' personal information does not become private just because we ban mobile phones in schools. It is better to learn how to use technology safely rather than totally ban it. Therefore, we should be looking at ways where mobile phones can be used effectively during some lessons including educating our students on social skills and safety strategies.

We need to trust our students and understand that in our world today, it is extremely difficult to get jobs if we do not have digital skills including using our mobile phones to connect with our organisation. This includes keeping their personal information safe and learning strategies to counter cyber bullying.

Whether we like it or not, technology is here to stay. Instead of pretending that a mobile phone ban in schools will have a positive impact on students' learning and mental health, it is better to face reality and support students to become more effective mobile phone users.

Reading and Viewing Activities

A: Word Level

1. List all the verbs you can see.

   [   ]

2. The verbs are written in the _____ tense because _____.
3. List all the nouns you can see.

   [   ]

4. The nouns tell us that the writer is writing about _____
5. List all the words the writer has used to persuade the reader.

   [   ]

6. How do you feel when you read these persuasive words _____?
7. List three arguments that the writer has used against the ban of mobile phones in schools:

Argument 1	
Argument 2	
Argument 3	

B: Sentence Level

Answer the questions using complete sentences.

1. What are the TWO main reasons the governments banned mobile phones in schools?
   a. _____
   b. _____
2. What is this argument trying to do?
   _____
3. Explain the main arguments given in the text against the statements below using your own words.

Students perform badly if they are allowed to use mobile phones at school.	
Students will be cyber bullied if they are allowed to use mobile phones at school.	

Complete the table below. Use ideas from the text. The first example has been completed for you.

Argument for mobile phone ban	Argument against mobile phone ban	<ul><li>Statistics</li><li>Expert opinion</li><li>Other facts or opinions</li></ul>
Students are distracted and perform badly.	During Covid lockdowns students used mobile phones for online schooling.	In 2021, the average ATAR score was 87.1%.

C: Text Level

Write TWO sentences to explain what each sub-heading is about. Then answer the two questions.

Introduction	
Student performance	
Cyber bullying	
Conclusion	
Think about how the writer has written about different things in each paragraph. 1. How does the writer use the paragraphs to write their arguments? 2. How will you use this idea to plan your own argument?	a. b.

Functional Grammar

	Describe	What?	Extra Information
the	modern	countries	around the world.
		mobile phones	
		students	
		schools	
		technology	
		computers	

D: Writing:

Choose ONE of the questions below. Use your answer to write a short argument

1. Do you think students should wear school uniforms when they come to school?
2. Do you think that school canteens should sell unhealthy food?

Part Two – Post Beginner Level – Argument

Genre 3, Text 2

Teacher's Notes: What is an Argument?

An argument is a type of writing that presents a position or viewpoint on a particular issue or topic, and provides evidence and reasoning to support that position. The purpose of an argument is to persuade the reader to understand, accept, and support the writer's point of view. Sometimes arguments may convince the reader to take a specific course of action.

There are many forms of arguments including essays, speeches, debates, and editorials. Arguments should have a clear structure so they are easy for readers to follow. The structure of an argument should include:

- Introduction – this outlines the topic, provides background information, and a summary of the evidence that may be presented.
- The thesis statement – one statement of the main argument.
- Body paragraphs – two to three paragraphs that provide:
    - examples
    - statistics
    - research
    - anecdotal and expert opinions
    - provide rebuttal to counter arguments that may arise
- Conclusion – restates the thesis and summarises the arguments.

When teaching how to write arguments to English as an Additional Language/Dialect (EAL/D) students, it is important to explicitly discuss:

- The use of persuasive language.
- How to do simple research to find statistics and expert opinions.
- Adding visual aids such as graphs, diagrams, illustrations, etc.

For EAL/D students, writing arguments can be a valuable tool for developing critical thinking, analysing simple data, and improving their communication skills. They also help EAL/D students to demonstrate how they can support their views with factual and anecdotal evidence. Arguments are an effective way to present objective observations and build academic writing skills.

Features of an Argument

- Clear and focused thesis statement/question.
- Clearly and logically organised – each fact, data, expert opinion should support the thesis statement.
- Evidence – statistics, expert opinion, examples, etc.
- Language features – persuasive language to convince the reader.
- Tone – objective and avoid personal attacks.
- Conclusion – summary of main points that support the thesis statement/question.

Text 2 – Argument

Is homework necessary?

Writing arguments can help EAL/D students explore the concepts of providing supporting evidence to strengthen their points of view. They lay the foundations for writing and other communication skills such as debates, oral presentations, and exploring social and political issues. Writing simple arguments at the post-beginner level allows students to experiment with fundamental skills for academic writing, presenting speeches, exploring pros and cons, and other non-fiction reports.

Genre 3 – Argument
Is homework necessary?

Word Bank

necessary	Do we need it?
creates	Starts
debate	Argument where some people say yes and others say no
wealthier	Have more money
inequality	Not equal or having the same types of things to help
pros and cons	Good and bad
conclude	Decide
educators	Teachers and other adults helping you at school
explore	Learn more about something
repetition	Doing the same thing a few times
discipline	Able to do something even if is hard or we do not like to do it
connection	A link joining everyone
reduce	Less time
resources	Things that can help with homework such as computers
requires	Needs
disadvantage	Have difficulties
discouraged	Do not feel like finishing what they have started
anxious	Very worried
crucial	Very important
quality	Something of high value – how good the homework is
quantity	Amount – how much homework
reinforce	Give more support
mindless	Boring

Model Text – Annotated for whole class discussion

Is homework necessary? (Title – tells us what our argument is about)

Introduction (Sub-heading or Paragraph Title – tells us what the paragraph is about) Is homework really necessary? The word homework quickly creates a debate amongst teachers and students. Some think that homework is important and necessary to support what students have learnt at school while others think that homework is a waste of time. According to the American Psychological Association (APA), "Kids from wealthier families have computers and parents to help with homework but kids from poorer families may have to work after school or not have parents at home to help". Therefore, homework can create the problem of inequality in the classroom. On the other hand, some studies show that homework helps students remember what they have learnt at school and therefore perform better at tests. In this argument, we are going to look at the pros and cons of homework and conclude whether homework is necessary.	• Thesis statement of the argument. • The first two or three sentences introduce the reader to the topic. • Expert opinion. • Counter arguments/persuasive language • The last sentence of the introduction tells the reader what this argument will do.
Pros of homework (Sub-heading or Paragraph Title – tells us what the paragraph is about) Firstly, we will look at the pros of doing homework. Many educators and parents believe that homework encourages students to practise what they have learnt at school. Sometimes, school hours are not enough for students to learn and understand new things, so homework gives them extra time to think and explore their work. In turn, this repetition creates discipline and allows students to develop good study skills and better grades. Another idea that supports homework is that it allows parents to take part in their children's education and understand what is going on at school. Therefore, the argument is that homework creates a connection between students, teachers, and parents. Some people also think that homework teaches students and parents how to manage their time and helps to reduce family screen time.	• Topic sentence • Persuasive language
Cons of homework (Sub-heading or Paragraph Title – tells us what the paragraph is about) On the other hand, many educators and parents feel that homework actually has a negative impact on students. For young children, homework can take away important play and family time.	• Topic sentence • Expert opinion • Counter arguments/persuasive language

In some homes, parents are unable to help their children due to language problems, lack of resources, working hours and so on. Not all families can afford computers and internet bills. Therefore, in today's world where homework often requires online research, students without access to technology are at a disadvantage. In these situations, homework can create many problems between students and their parents. This may lead to students feeling discouraged or anxious about homework.

Another argument against homework is that some students spend time on extra activities such as clubs and sports after school. Adding homework to this creates stress and takes away their time to socialise with their friends and family. Even adults cannot keep working for so many hours a day.

Conclusion (Sub-heading or Paragraph Title – tells us what the paragraph is about)

- Topic sentence
- Counter arguments/persuasive language

In conclusion, we can see that homework has many pros and cons and not an easy question to answer. It is important to understand that homework impacts students the most. Therefore, it is crucial for parents and teachers to ask for their opinions and suggestions when it comes to homework.

Homework should add to students' learning or completing unfinished work. Mostly, students must be able to complete their homework on their own without giving up on family time. Teachers should also understand that some parents are unable to help with homework. After school homework clubs may be the answer to this problem.

Finally, providing quality over quantity is something teachers can aim for. Completing short assignment that reinforce what students have learnt at school will allow students to improve their learning instead of just completing hours of mindless worksheets. From the pros and cons above, we can see that younger children may not need any homework whereas secondary school students may need some homework in order to improve their time management and study skills.

Discussion questions:

1. What are we writing?
2. What is this argument about?
3. What does the title tell us? Do you think it is important to have a title/ Why?
4. How do sub-headings help us?
5. What are the words we use to help us persuade our readers? How do these words help us convey our message?
6. How is this argument presented?

Unlocking Genre 89

Model Text – Non-Annotated

Introduction

Is homework really necessary? The word homework quickly creates a debate amongst teachers and students. Some think that homework is important and necessary to support what students have learnt at school while others think that homework is a waste of time.

According to the American Psychological Association (APA), "Kids from wealthier families have computers and parents to help with homework but kids from poorer families may have to work after school or not have parents at home to help". Therefore, homework can create the problem of inequality in the classroom.

On the other hand, some studies show that homework helps students remember what they have learnt at school and therefore perform better at tests. In this argument, we are going to look at the pros and cons of homework and conclude whether homework is necessary.

Pros of homework

Firstly, we will look at the pros of doing homework. Many educators and parents believe that homework encourages students to practise what they have learnt at school. Sometimes, school hours are not enough for students to learn and understand new things, so homework gives them extra time to think and explore their work. In turn, this repetition creates discipline and allows students to develop good study skills and better grades.

Another idea that supports homework is that it allows parents to take part in their children's education and understand what is going on at school. Therefore, the argument is that homework creates a connection between students, teachers, and parents. Some people also think that homework teaches students and parents how to manage their time and helps to reduce family screen time.

Cons of homework

On the other hand, many educators and parents feel that homework actually has a negative impact on students. For young children, homework can take away important play and family time.

In some homes, parents are unable to help their children due to language problems, lack of resources, working hours and so on. Not all families can afford computers and internet bills. Therefore, in today's world where homework often requires online research, students without access to technology are at a disadvantage. In these situations, homework can create many problems between students and their parents. This may lead to students feeling discouraged or anxious about homework.

Another argument against homework is that some students spend time on extra activities such as clubs and sports after school. Adding homework to this creates stress and takes away their time to socialise with their friends and family. Even adults cannot keep working for so many hours a day.

Conclusion

In conclusion, we can see that homework has many pros and cons and not an easy question to answer. It is important to understand that homework impacts students the most. Therefore, it is crucial for parents and teachers to ask for their opinions and suggestions when it comes to homework.

Homework should add to students' learning or completing unfinished work. Mostly, students must be able to complete their homework on their own without giving up on family time. Teachers should also understand that some parents are unable to help with homework. After school homework clubs may be the answer to this problem.

Finally, providing quality over quantity is something teachers can aim for. Completing short assignment that reinforce what students have learnt at school will allow students to improve their learning instead of just completing hours of mindless worksheets. From the pros and cons above, we can see that younger children may not need any homework whereas secondary school students may need some homework in order to improve their time management and study skills.

Reading and Viewing Activities

A: Word Level

1. List all the verbs you can see.

   [   ]

2. The verbs are written in the _____ tense because _____.
3. List all the nouns you can see.

   [   ]

4. The nouns tell us that the writer is writing about _____
5. List all the words the writer has used to persuade the reader.

   [   ]

6. What do pros and cons do? _____
7. How do pros and cons help with the conclusion? _____

B: Sentence Level

Answer the questions using complete sentences.

1. What is this argument looking at?
   _____

2. Why do you think the writer wants to explore both pros and cons for this argument?
   _____

3. List three pros and three cons about homework that the writer has presented in this argument.

Pros	Cons

Complete the table below. Write a pro or con for each statement. Use ideas from the text. The first two examples have been completed for you. Use the clues to help you.

Pros	Cons
Homework supports what students have learnt at school.	**Homework is a waste of time.**
Homework gives student extra time to practice their school work.	Homework can take away play time.
Homework creates good study skills.	*Clue – bad feelings
*Clue - connections	Parents do not have time to help their children with homework.
All homework helps all students get good grades.	*Clue – quality over quantity

Unlocking Genre 91

C: Text Level

Write ONE sentences to explain what each sub-heading is about. Provide an example for each explanation. Then answer the two questions.

Introduction	
Pros of homework	
Cons of homework	
Conclusion	
Think about how the writer has written this argument. a. How does the writer create an interest using the title? b. How does the writer present this argument? c. How will you use this idea to plan your own argument?	a. b. c.

Functional Grammar

	Describe	What?	Extra Information
the	English	homework	was very difficult.
		families	
		test	
		grades	
		parents	
		day	

D: Writing:

Choose ONE of the questions below. Use your answer to write a short argument using the pros and cons method.

1. Is eating meat bad for our health?
2. Is social media important?

Unlocking Genre   92

PART THREE:
English as an Additional Language/Dialect (EAL/D) – Intermediate/Developing Level

Who Are Post Beginner/Emerging EAL/D Students?

Intermediate EAL/D students have moved beyond the beginner and emerging stages of language acquisition and are beginning to learn a new language. Students at this level are beginning to demonstrate more control in using English in various social and academic contexts.

Challenges Faced by Intermediate/Developing EAL/D Students

Intermediate EAL/D students face a set of challenges as they aim to progress from proficiency to fluency:

- Expanding Vocabulary: Continuing to build their vocabulary and make sense of more specialised terms for various subjects.
- Complex Grammar: Mastering advanced grammar rules, including tenses, complex sentence structures, and idiomatic expressions.
- Academic Language Skills: Developing the language abilities needed for academic success, such as research and writing.

Strategies to Support Intermediate/Developing EAL/D Students

To help intermediate EAL students advance to fluency, consider the following strategies:

- Explicit teaching: Continue teaching the features and register of English for different contexts.
- Academic Language: Offer guidance and support in academic writing, research, and presentation skills.
- Subject specific vocabulary: Time to start introducing more subject specific vocabulary.
- Clear modelling: Model planning and editing strategies.
- Assessment criteria: Explicitly discuss assessment criteria using checklists and rubrics.

Genres and some Australian Curriculum links for this level:

Genre	Topic	Australian Curriculum link
Historical Recount	Ancient Egypt	<ul><li>using a growing range of strategies for planning and refining work, including editing for correct simple tenses, common punctuation, and a variety of simple and compound sentences. (ACEEA179)</li><li>using first-person and third-person narration (ACEEA172)</li><li>identifying common variations of language and structure across different mediums. (ACEEA170)</li></ul>
	The First Fleet	<ul><li>using a growing range of strategies for planning and refining work, including editing for correct simple tenses, common punctuation, and a variety of simple and compound sentences. (ACEEA179)</li><li>using first-person and third-person narration (ACEEA172)</li><li>identifying common variations of language and structure across different mediums. (ACEEA170)</li></ul>

Descriptive Report	Our Solar System	• using a growing range of strategies for planning and refining work, including editing for correct simple tenses, common punctuation, and a variety of simple and compound sentences. (ACEEA179) • employing ICT and investigative strategies to locate information from other sources. (ACEEA165)
	Human Respiratory System	• using a growing range of strategies for planning and refining work, including editing for correct simple tenses, common punctuation, and a variety of simple and compound sentences. (ACEEA179) • identifying common variations of language and structure across different mediums. (ACEEA170) • employing ICT and investigative strategies to locate information from other sources. (ACEEA165)
Book Report	The Little Refugee	• describing characters and settings presented in literary texts and recounting plot details (ACEEA160) • identifying dialogue, and first-person and third-person narration used in literary texts (ACEEA167) • using first-person and third-person narration (ACEEA172) • identifying emotive language and sociocultural references in a growing range of situations (ACEEA163)
	The Rabbits	• identifying and responding to the main ideas in a range of familiar texts (ACEEA162) • identifying emotive language and sociocultural references in a growing range of situations (ACEEA163) • using first-person and third-person narration (ACEEA172)

Part Three – Intermediate/Developing Level – Historical Recount

Genre 1, Text 1

Teacher's Notes: What is a Historical Recount?

A historical recount is a type of writing that describes past events or experiences. The purpose is to inform or educate the reader about historical events, people, and cultures. Historical recounts can take many forms, such as biographies, autobiographies, diaries, letters, memoirs, and history textbooks.

Historical recounts are an important genre that teaches students about the past and can help them develop critical thinking and analytical skills. They can also provide insights into current events and issues by showing how historical events have shaped the world we live in today.

For English as an Additional Language/Dialect (EAL/D) students, historical recounts can be a valuable tool for developing contextual and analytical skills, as well as for communicating historical information in a clear and accessible way. They are an effective way to build objective research and academic writing skills.

Features of a Historical Recount

- Accurate and factual – based on reliable sources.
- Chronological order.
- Clearly and logically organised – may include heading, sub-headings, images with captions, conclusion etc.
- Objective language – more facts, less personal opinions.
- Language features – adjectives and adverbs to create more depth.
- Contextualised - provide context of social, economic, and political factors.

Text 1 – Historical Recount

Ancient Egypt

Researching and recounting ancient civilisations can help EAL/D students improve their research skills and learn about the history of ancient cultures that have influenced the modern world through their languages, art, inventions and social practices. This will help set them up for future historic exploration and is an example of how we can teach English using cross-curricular subject areas. Writing simple historical recounts at the intermediate level allows students to experiment with fundamental skills for academic research and non-fiction work.

Genre 1 – Historical Recount
Ancient Egypt

Word Bank

civilisation	A group of humans that have languages, culture, laws, and so on to progress. We are now a modern civilisation.
desert	An area of land that is dry and covered with sand.
flooded	Covered in water.
fertile	Land where it is easy to grow fruits and vegetables.
Invent/invention	To make or create something new.
solar calendar	Calendar that follows the movement of the sun.
carved	To cut or write on something hard such as a rock.
tombs	A place built to bury the dead. It is usually underground.
preserved	To stop something from rotting.
discover/discovery/discovered	To find something new.
rags	Small pieces of old cloth
linen	A type of cloth.
amulets	A small piece of jewellery that is thought to protect from danger.
magic spells	Words that are thought to have magic.
worshipped	Prayed
kneaded	Pressed with hands.
descent	Fall
invaded	Take over land
glimpses	A little peek
BCE	Before Common Era

Unlocking Genre   96

Model Text – Annotated for whole class discussion

Structure	Historical Recount	Language Features
Title	Ancient Egypt	Title – tells us what our recount is about.
Introduction We are introducing the recount.	Ancient Egypt was one of the greatest and most powerful civilisations that began about 5000 years ago. It started when people began living in mud houses and farming along the River Nile. The rest of Egypt was a desert. The river flooded the land around it every year. This provided a fertile soil and enough water to grow crops, vegetables, and fruits. They also grew a plant called papyrus that allowed them to have something to write on. During the floods, when they could not farm, the farmers spent their time doing other important things such as putting up buildings, and recording their lives on papyrus. The communities along the river kept growing until they became villages. We now know that the Ancient Egyptians were very good at farming, constructing buildings, and inventing many amazing things.	Sub-heading or Paragraph Title – tells us what the paragraph is about. The first two or three sentences introduce the reader to the topic. Past tense. The first paragraph informs us WHAT it is, WHEN it happened, WHY it happened. The second paragraph gives us more information about the people who lived then and what they were famous for.
Ancient Egyptian Inventions We are going into a new sub-heading	Ancient Egyptians invented many things that are still helping our lives today. Our modern calendar is based on the ancient solar calendar designed by Egyptians. They also created paper from the papyrus plant and used it to develop a writing system called hieroglyphs. It had more than 700 symbols. We can still see hieroglyphs carved into many temples and tombs recording names, dates, battles, and even instructions for the afterlife. These symbols are closest to the modern English alphabet. The most famous evidence to these writing is the Rosetta Stone that was discovered in 1799. We now know that they also made many things that we still use today such as pens, locks and keys, and even toothpaste! Many historians think that division and multiplication were also first developed by Ancient Egyptians as it would have been impossible to build the pyramids without using mathematical measurements.	Sub-heading or Paragraph Title – tells us what the paragraph is about. Past tense. The first sentence links with the sub-heading. The following sentences list important inventions that influenced modern life. Evidence to support the recount. Popular expert opinion.

Afterlife We are going into a new sub-heading	The Ancient Egyptians believed that there is a never-ending life after death. So, they preserved dead bodies of important people liked their rulers; kings and queens known as pharaohs. This was done through the process of mummification and they built special tombs to bury them. These tombs were filled with their favourite things and often included precious stones, jewellery, gold and so on. Some pharaohs made their people build pyramids for their tombs. The most famous discovery was the tomb of the young King Tutankhamun or King Tut. This is because his tomb was discovered in 1922 without much damage and almost all the treasures inside. The pyramids built by Ancient Egyptians around 4000 years ago are still standing today.	Sub-heading or Paragraph Title – tells us what the paragraph is about. Past tense. The first sentence links with the sub-heading. Also explains what they did – linked to the sub-heading Explains the process. Provides some details to support the explanation. Historical evidence
Mummification Process We are going into a new sub-heading. This one is a continuation of the sub-heading before this.	The Ancient Egyptians followed a process to mummify dead bodies. First, they would wash the body with wine and water from the Nile. Then they would remove the heart, liver, lungs, intestines, and stomach. They cleaned the organs and put them into four special jars. The heart was put back into the body as it was considered the most important part of human intelligence. They would throw the brain away, as it was regarded unimportant and useless! After that, they used a special salt called natron to close up all the holes and cover the body. They left the body in the salt for forty days so it could completely dry out. When the body was completely dry, they removed the salt and stuffed the body with spices, plants, and small rags for it to keep its human shape. Finally, they wrapped the body in linen, added amulets and said magic *spells* to protect it before putting it in a coffin. These linen wrappings were sometimes over a kilometre long! 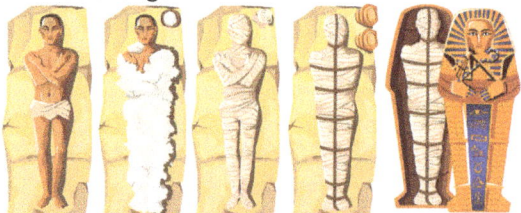 *The Ancient Egyptians followed a process to mummify bodies.*	Sub-heading or Paragraph Title – tells us what the paragraph is about. Past tense. The first sentence links with the sub-heading. Explains the process. Includes details of the process. Explanation of why this was done. Caption

Interesting Facts about Ancient Egyptians New sub-heading. Added to make the recount more interesting.	• They worshipped more than 2000 gods and goddesses. • They sometimes kneaded dough for their bread using their feet. • They believed that cats were magical creatures and mummified them when they died. • Both men and women wore makeup. • Cleopatra was the last pharaoh. *The Ancient Egyptians had more than 2000 gods and goddesses.*	Sub-heading or Paragraph Title – tells us what the paragraph is about. Past tense. Not more than five. Dot points and short sentences. Caption.
Conclusion Sub-heading	The Ancient Egyptian civilisation began its descent around 1000 BCE when they were divided by war between priests and pharaohs. They were then invaded by many of their neighbours and other European armies. Although modern Egypt is ruled by a president, not a pharaoh, and has a main religion and language, glimpses of Ancient Egypt are still all around in the pyramids, ancient writings, and inventions that still matter today.	Sub-heading or Paragraph Title – tells us what the paragraph is about and signals that we are coming to the end of the report. Past tense. Present tense – current. The first sentence tells us that the civilisation was coming to an end. Events that ended the civilisation. Contrasting modern Egypt to ancient. Linking to the beginning paragraph.

Discussion questions:

1. Where do you think we can find information about these types of topics?
2. What does the title tell us? Do you think it is important to have a title/ Why?
3. How do sub-headings help us?
4. Have you seen pictures of ancient Egypt?
5. Why do you think the ancient Egyptian civilisation is an important one?
6. What do you think is the oldest civilisation of your home country?
7. Discuss what quotation marks are ("mud houses"). When do we use them? Why do we use them?

Model Text – Non-Annotated

Ancient Egypt

Introduction

Ancient Egypt was one of the greatest and most powerful civilisations that began about 5000 years ago. It started when people began living in mud houses and farming along the River Nile. The rest of Egypt was a desert. The river flooded the land around it every year. This provided a fertile soil and enough water to grow crops, vegetables, and fruits. They also grew a plant called papyrus that allowed them to have something to write on.

During the floods, when they could not farm, the farmers spent their time doing other important things such as constructing buildings, and recording their lives on papyrus. The communities along the river kept growing until they became villages. We now know that the Ancient Egyptians were very good at farming, constructing buildings, and inventing many amazing things.

Ancient Egyptian Inventions

Ancient Egyptians invented many things that are still helping our lives today. Our modern calendar is based on the ancient solar calendar designed by Egyptians. They also created paper from the papyrus plant and used it to develop a writing system called hieroglyphs. It had more than 700 symbols. We can still see hieroglyphs carved into many temples and tombs recording names, dates, battles, and even instructions for the afterlife. These symbols are closest to the modern English alphabet. The most famous evidence to these writing is the Rosetta Stone that was discovered in 1799.

We now know that they also made many things that we still use today such as pens, locks and keys, and even toothpaste! Many historians think that division and multiplication were also first developed by Ancient Egyptians as it would have been impossible to build the pyramids without using mathematical measurements.

Afterlife

The Ancient Egyptians believed that there is a never-ending life after death. So, they preserved dead bodies of important people liked their rulers; kings and queens known as pharaohs. This was done through the process of mummification and built special tombs to bury them. These tombs were filled with their favourite things and often included precious stones, jewellery, gold and so on. Some pharaohs made their people build pyramids for their tombs. The most famous discovery was the tomb of the young King Tutankhamun or King Tut. This is because his tomb was discovered in 1922 without much damage and almost all the treasures inside. The pyramids built by Ancient Egyptians around 4000 years ago are still standing today.

Mummification Process

The Ancient Egyptians followed a process to mummify dead bodies. First, they would wash the body with wine and water from the Nile. Then they would remove the heart, liver, lungs, intestines, and stomach. They cleaned the organs and put them into four special jars. The heart was put back into the body as it was considered the most important part of human intelligence. They would throw the brain away, as it was considered unimportant and useless!

After that, they used a special salt called natron to close up all the holes and cover the body. They left the body in the salt for 40 days so it could completely dry out. When the body was completely dry, they removed the salt and stuffed the body with spices, plants, and small rags for it to keep its human shape. Finally, they wrapped the body with linen, added amulets and said magic spells to protect it before putting it in a coffin. These linen wrappings were sometimes over a kilometre long!

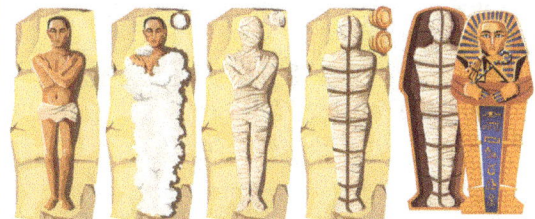

The Ancient Egyptians followed a process to mummify bodies.

Interesting facts about Ancient Egyptians
- They worshipped more than 2000 gods and goddesses.
- They sometimes kneaded dough for their bread using their feet.
- They believed that cats were magical creatures and mummified them when they died.
- Both men and women wore makeup.
- Cleopatra was the last pharaoh.

The Ancient Egyptians had more than 2000 gods and goddesses.

Conclusion

The Ancient Egyptian civilisation began its descent around 1000 BCE when they were divided by war between priests and pharaohs. They were then invaded by many of their neighbours and other European armies. Although modern Egypt in ruled by a president, not a pharaoh, and has a main religion and language, glimpses of Ancient Egypt are still all around in the pyramids, ancient writings, and inventions that still matter today.

Reading and Viewing Activities

A: Word Level

1. List all the verbs you can see.

   [ ]

3. The verbs are written in the _____ tense because _____.
4. Why do you think we use the word 'the' when we write about Ancient Egyptians?

5. List FIVE words or phrases that tell you this passage is about something that has happened in the past. Give a reason why you think so. One example has been done for you.

Word/phrase from the passage	My reason
"began about 5000 years ago"	this tells me that the Ancient Egypt civilisation started a long time ago.

6. Why do you think we use " " (quotation marks) when we copy words or phrases from the passage?
   _____

7. List ONE new word you learnt from each paragraph. What does it mean?

Paragraph	New word	Meaning
1		
2		
3		
4		
5		
6		

8. What did you do to find the meaning of new words?
   _____

9. What do these numbers tell us?

5000	
700	
1799	
1922	
4000	
40	
2000	
1000 BCE	

Unlocking Genre   102

B: Sentence Level

Answer the questions using complete sentences.

1. Why do we need an introduction?
   _____

2. What is this recount about?
   _____

3. List three examples of what Ancient Egyptians did.
   a. _____
   b. _____
   c. _____

4. Why do we consider Ancient Egypt as "one of the greatest civilisations"?
   _____

5. Rearrange the mummification process in the table below by writing numbers 1 – in the boxes next to the sentences. The first one has been done for you. Explain what helped you to do this.

Clean the organs and put them into four special jars.	
Put in a coffin.	
Wash the body with wine and water from the Nile.	1
Stuff the body with spices, plants, and small rags.	
Put the heart back into the body and throw the brain away.	
Wrap the body with linen.	
Remove the heart, liver, lungs, intestines, and stomach.	
Leave the body covered in salt for 40 days.	
Explanation: What helped you to rearrange the process in the correct order?	

Write your own beginning sentence for each these sub-headings.

Sub-heading	Sentence from the passage	My own sentence
1 - Introduction	Ancient Egypt was one of the greatest and most powerful civilisations that began about 5000 years ago.	
2 - Ancient Egyptian Inventions	Ancient Egyptians invented many things that are still helping our lives today.	
3 - Afterlife	The ancient Egyptians believed that there is a never-ending life after death.	
4 - Mummification Process	The ancient Egyptians followed a process to mummify dead bodies.	
5 - Conclusion	The Ancient Egyptian civilisation began its descent around 1000 BCE when they were divided by war between priests and pharaohs.	

Unlocking Genre

C: Text Level

Write TWO sentences to show what each sub-heading is about. Then answer the two questions.

Sub-heading 1	
Sub-heading 2	
Sub-heading 3	
Sub-heading 4	
Sub-heading 5	
Sub-heading 6	
Think about how the writer has written about different things under each sub-heading. a. How does each sub-heading and the information under that connect to the title? b. How will you use this idea in your own writing?	a. b.

Functional Grammar

	Describe	What?	Extra Information
an	ancient	civilisation	that gave us many inventions.
		desert	
		river	
		papyrus	
		pyramids	
		pharaohs	
		tomb	
		mummy	
		language	

D: Writing

Choose ONE of the civilisations below. Write your own Historical Recount about it. Use the sub-headings to help you plan.

Ancient Mesopotamia
Ancient China
Ancient India

Title	
Introduction	
Inventions	
Beliefs	
Interesting facts	
Conclusion	

Unlocking Genre 104

Part Three – Intermediate/Developing Level – Historical Recount

Genre 1, Text 2

Teacher's Notes: What is a Historical Recount?

A historical recount is a type of writing that describes past events or experiences. The purpose is to inform or educate the reader about historical events, people, and cultures. Historical recounts can take many forms, such as biographies, autobiographies, diaries, letters, memoirs, and history textbooks.

Historical recounts are an important genre that teaches students about the past and can help them develop critical thinking and analytical skills. They can also provide insights into current events and issues by showing how historical events have shaped the world we live in today.

For English as an Additional Language/Dialect (EAL/D) students, historical recounts can be a valuable tool for developing contextual and analytical skills, as well as for communicating historical information in a clear and accessible way. They are an effective way to build objective research and academic writing skills.

Features of a Historical Recount

- Accurate and factual – based on reliable sources.
- Chronological order.
- Clearly and logically organised – may include heading, sub-headings, images with captions, conclusion etc.
- Objective language – more facts, less personal opinions.
- Language features – adjectives and adverbs to create more depth.
- Contextualised - provide context of social, economic, and political factors.

Text 2 – Historical Recount

The First Fleet

Researching and recounting The First Fleet can help EAL/D students improve their research skills and learn about the history of the country including the colonisation of the Australian Indigenous people. This will help set them up for future historic exploration and is an example of how we can teach English using cross-curricular subject areas. Writing simple historical recounts at the intermediate level allows students to experiment with fundamental skills for academic research and non-fiction work.

Genre 1 – Historical Recount
The First Fleet

Word Bank

fleet	A group of ships.
settlers	A person who has arrived in a new country and wants to live there.
consider	Think.
represents	What something means.
occupation	Take over someone's home.
convicts	Someone who has done something wrong by the law.
prison	A place where convicts are kept.
Aboriginal people	The first people who live on a land.
curious	Interested
harmony	Taking care of each other.
construct	Build or make.
wonder/wondered	Think about something without knowing the answer.
protect/protected	Keep someone or something safe.
culture	The way a group of people live. This includes their languages, beliefs, religions, clothes, and food.
cargo	Things that are put in ships to take them somewhere else.
male	Boy/man.
female	Girl/woman.
modern/modernisation	New things that were not there before – telephones, roads, trains…
ancestral	Coming from people who lived a long time before.
sovereignty	Belongs to, have power to rule…
ceded	Give without force.

Unlocking Genre   106

Model Text – Annotated for whole class discussion

Structure	Historical Recount	Language Features
Title	The First Fleet	Title – tells us what our recount is about.
Introduction We are introducing the recount.	The First Fleet is the name given to the 11 ships that brought the first white settlers to Australia. They arrived at Sydney Cove on 26th January 1788. This day is celebrated as Australia Day. However, Aboriginal people consider the day as Invasion Day as it represents the occupation of their land. Most of the people in these ships were convicts that were being sent out of England because the prisons in England were getting too full. The captain of the fleet was Captain Arthur Phillip. It took them eight months of sailing from England to finally reach Australia.	Sub-heading or Paragraph Title – tells us what the paragraph is about. Past tense. Present tense – still the same facts. The first two or three sentences introduce the reader to the topic. WHAT it is, WHEN it happened, WHY it happened. Historical fact.
First Contact We are going into a new sub-heading	At that time, the Aboriginal people of the Eora nation lived in Sydney Cove. They were curious and a little afraid of the newcomers. For more than 50 000 years, Aboriginal people lived in harmony with the land. They moved around according to the seasons to hunt and gather food. They only took what they needed and did not construct fences or buildings. They also did not plant crops or have farm animals. They wondered why the white people wanted to take their land and turn them into farms protected by fences. The British did not take the time to understand the Aboriginal people's history, culture, language, or way of life. They believed that the land did not belong to anyone and was free for them to take and use as they pleased. There were many fights and killings.	Sub-heading or Paragraph Title – tells us what the paragraph is about. Past tense. What happened – linked to the sub-heading. Who was already there. Additional information about who was already there.
Interesting facts about The First Fleet New sub-heading. Added to make the recount more interesting.	• They travelled as far as 24 000 km to reach Australia. • The youngest convict on the fleet was Mary Wade, aged 9. • The First Fleet also carried other cargo such as farm animals and plant seeds. • The male convicts were asked to build prisons and other places as part of their punishment. • The female convicts worked as servants.	Sub-heading or Paragraph Title – tells us what the paragraph is about. Past tense. Historical facts linked to the sub-heading.
Conclusion Sub-heading	The First Fleet included prisoners and free people who wanted to start a new life. While they were the beginning of the modernisation of Australia, they also caused a lot of suffering and pain for the Aboriginal people. They are still fighting for the ownership of their ancestral land. According to them, "sovereignty was never ceded", meaning that they never gave away their land, it was taken by force. Many white Australians also support this statement.	Sub-heading or Paragraph Title – tells us what the paragraph is about and signals that we are coming to the end of the report. Past tense. Present tense – current situation. The first sentence tells us who came along in the first fleet – linking to title. Linking back to the introduction. Current situation.

Discussion questions:

1. Where do you think we can find information about this topic?
2. What does the title tell us? Do you think it is important to have a title/ Why?
3. How do sub-headings help us?
4. Have you heard about the First Fleet?
5. Why do you think this information is important?
6. What else do you know about the history of Australia?
7. How can we understand the meaning of "sovereignty was never ceded" from reading the sentence? Look at the words that come after this phrase.

Model Text – Non-Annotated

The First Fleet

Introduction

The First Fleet is the name given to the 11 ships that brought the first white settlers to Australia. They arrived at Sydney Cove on 26th January 1788. This day is celebrated as Australia Day. However, Aboriginal people consider the day as Invasion Day as it represents the occupation of their land.

Most of the people in these ships were convicts that were being sent out of England because the prisons in England were getting too full. The captain of the fleet was Captain Arthur Phillip. It took them eight months of sailing from England to finally reach Australia.

First Contact

At that time, the Aboriginal people of the Eora nation lived in Sydney Cove. They were curious and a little afraid of the newcomers. For more than 50 000 years, Aboriginal people lived in harmony with the land. They moved around according to the seasons to hunt and gather food. They only took what they needed and did not construct fences or buildings. They also did not plant crops or have farm animals.

They wondered why the white people wanted to take their land and turn them into farms protected by fences. The British did not take the time to understand the Aboriginal people's history, culture, language, or way of life. They believed that the land did not belong to anyone and was free for them to take and use as they pleased. There were many fights and killings.

Interesting facts about The First Fleet

- They travelled as far as 24 000 km to reach Australia.
- The youngest convict on the fleet was Mary Wade, aged 9.
- The First Fleet also carried other cargo such as farm animals and plant seeds.
- The male convicts were asked to build prisons and other places as part of their punishment.
- The female convicts worked as servants.

Conclusion

The First Fleet included prisoners and free people who wanted to start a new life. While they were the beginning of the modernisation of Australia, they also caused a lot of suffering and pain for the Aboriginal people. They are still fighting for the ownership of their ancestral land. According to them, "sovereignty was never ceded", meaning that they never gave away their land, it was taken by force.

Reading and Viewing Activities
A: Word Level

1. List all the verbs you can see.

   [   ]

2. The verbs are written in the _____ tense because _____.
3. Why do you think we use the word 'the' and capital letters when we write about the First Fleet?
4. List FIVE words or phrases that tell you this passage is about something that has happened in the past. Give a reason why you think so. One example has been done for you.

Word/phrase from the passage	My reason
"on January 26 1788"	We are now in the year 2023, so the year 1788 was a long time ago.

5. Why do you think we use " " (quotation marks) when we copy words or phrases from the passage?
   _____

6. List ONE new word you learnt from each sub-heading. What does it mean? Write your own sentence using the new word.

Paragraph	New word	Meaning	Write your own sentence using the word.
1			
2			
3			
4			

7. What did you do to find the meaning of new words?
   _____

8. What do these numbers tell us? The first one has been done for you.

11	The number of ships in the First Fleet.
26	
1788	
50 000	
24 000	
9	

Unlocking Genre

B: Sentence Level

Answer the questions using complete sentences.

1. Why do we need an introduction?
   _____

2. What is this recount about?
   _____

3. List three sentences from the passage that tell you how the Aboriginal people felt about the first white settlers.
   a. _____
   b. _____
   c. _____

4. Look at the beginning of the second sub-heading. What does the phrase "at that time" refer to?
   a. _____

   b. What do these interesting facts tell you? One has been done for you.

They travelled as far as 24 000 km to reach Australia.	
The youngest convict on the fleet was Mary Wade, aged 9.	This tells me that even children were punished and made to leave England.
The First Fleet also carried other cargo such as farm animals and plant seeds.	1
The male convicts were asked to build prisons and other places as part of their punishment.	
The female convicts worked as servants.	

Write your own beginning sentence for each these sub-headings.

Sub-heading	Sentence from the passage	My own sentence
1 - Introduction	The First Fleet is the name given to the 11 ships that brought the first white settlers to Australia.	
2 - First Contact	At that time, the Aboriginal people of the Eora nation lived in Sydney Cove.	
4 - Conclusion	The First Fleet included prisoners and free people who wanted to start a new life.	

C: Text Level

Write TWO sentences to show what each sub-heading is about. Then answer the two questions.

Sub-heading 1	
Sub-heading 2	
Sub-heading 3	
Sub-heading 4	
Sub-heading 5	
Sub-heading 6	
Think about how the writer has written about different things under each sub-heading. a. How does each sub-heading and the information under that connect to the title? b. How will you use this idea in your own writing?	a. b.

Functional Grammar

	Describe	What?	Extra Information
the	white	settlers	came in ships.
		land	
		convicts	
		food	
		crops	
		animals	
		language	
		cargo	
		servants	

D: Writing

Choose ONE of the events below. Write your own Historical Recount about it. Use the sub-headings to help you plan.

Sorry Day
Naidoc Week
Australia Day

Title	
Introduction - What is _____? - When was the first time ____ was celebrated/recognized/remembered?	
Why is _____ celebrated/recognized/remembered?	
How is _____ celebrated/recognized/remembered?	
3 Interesting facts about _____	
Conclusion	

Part Three – Intermediate/Developing Level – Descriptive Report

Genre 2, Text 1

Teacher's Notes: What is a Descriptive Report?

A descriptive report provides a detailed and objective description of a person, place, object, event, or phenomenon. The purpose of a descriptive report is to give the reader a clear and comprehensive understanding of the subject being described.

For English as an Additional Language/Dialect (EAL/D) students, descriptive reports can be a valuable tool for developing contextual and analytical skills, as well as for communicating scientific information in a clear and accessible way. They are an effective way to build objective research and academic writing skills.

Features of a Descriptive Report

- Accurate and factual – based on reliable sources.
- Clearly and logically organised – may include heading, sub-headings, images with captions, conclusion etc.
- Objective language – more facts, less personal opinions.
- Language features – e.g., adjectives and adverbs to create more depth.
- Contextualised - provide context of events, processes, objects being described.

Text 1 – Descriptive Report

Our Solar System

Researching and reporting about Our Solar System allows students to connect with our current advances in space travel. It also allows a broader perspective of the universe we know and what is necessary for life. Writing a descriptive report about our Solar System can help EAL/D students connect with space exploration through an exciting topic. This will help set them up for future descriptive report writing and is an example of how we can teach English using cross-curricular subject areas. Writing simple descriptive reports at the intermediate level allows students to experiment with fundamental skills for academic research and non-fiction work.

Part Three, Genre 2 – Descriptive Report
Our Solar System

Word Bank

collection	A few different things grouped together.
asteroids	Rocks floating in space.
located	Where they are.
extremely	very
orbit	Path around something.
gravity	Strong pull
dwarf	small
atmosphere	The gases surrounding the planets including earth.
phenomenon	Something that is amazing that we cannot really explain.

Model Text – Annotated for whole class discussion

Structure	Descriptive Report	Language Features
Title	Our Solar System	Title – tells us what we are describing
Introduction We are introducing the topic.	Our solar system is the collection of planets, moons, asteroids, and comets that orbit around the Sun. It is about 4.6 billion years old and located in the Milky Way galaxy. Although space is extremely large and we do not know everything about it, we have a lot information about our solar system.	Sub-heading or Paragraph Title – tells us what the paragraph is about. Present tense. The first two sentences introduce the reader to the topic.
The Sun We are going into a new sub-heading	The sun is the largest object in the centre of our solar system. However, the sun is not a planet. It is a star that is very bright and hot. All the planets orbit around the sun. It takes about 8 minutes for the light from the sun to reach earth. The light and heat from the sun allow things to live, grow, and survive on planet Earth. Without the sun, there will be no life on our planet.	Sub-heading or Paragraph Title – tells us what the paragraph is about. Present tense. Linked to the sub-heading. More information about the sub-heading. Linking the next sub-heading to this one.
The Planets We are going into a new sub-heading	There are eight planets in the solar system. They are Mercury, Venus, Earth, Mars, Jupiter, Saturn, Uranus, and Neptune. Pluto was once considered the ninth planet, but it was changed to a dwarf planet in 2006. All the planets move around the sun. The table below shows how the planets are different from each other:	Sub-heading or Paragraph Title – tells us what the paragraph is about. Present tense. Past tense – linking to something that happened in the past. Linked to the sub-heading. More information about the sub-heading. Using a table to break down differences helps the reader understand better.

	Mercury	<ul><li>Closest to the sun.</li><li>The smallest planet in the solar system.</li><li>Does not have a moon.</li><li>The side facing the sun is very hot (426.7 degrees Celsius).</li><li>The side away from the sun is very cold (-173 degrees Celsius)</li><li>Does not have an atmosphere.</li></ul>
	Venus	<ul><li>Second planet from the sun.</li><li>A little smaller than earth.</li><li>The hottest planet because it has a very thick atmosphere.</li><li>Too hot for life.</li><li>Does not have a moon.</li></ul>
	Earth	<ul><li>We live here!</li><li>Third planet from the sun.</li><li>The only planet we know that has water on 71% of its surface.</li><li>Has one moon.</li></ul>

Unlocking Genre 115

		- Takes 365 days to rotate around the sun. - Atmosphere has the perfect ingredients – 78% nitrogen, 21% oxygen, 1% other gasses – allows us to breathe.	
	Mars	- Fourth planet from the sun. - It is called the red planet because of iron on its surface. - Has large volcanoes and deep valleys. - We think that there may be water on Mars. - Colder than earth.	
	Jupiter	- Fifth planet from the sun. - Largest planet in the solar system. - Has 63 moons so far. - It is made up of gasses.	
	Saturn	- Sixth planet from the sun. - Has a ring around it. - It is the second largest planet in our solar system. - Has 82 moons so far. - It is a very cold planet.	
	Uranus	- Seventh planet from the sun. - A cold planet – we call it an ice giant. - Four times bigger than earth. - Has 27 moons so far.	
	Neptune	- Eighth planet from the sun. - It is called the blue planet. - The furthest away from the sun. - Very cold planet. - It has 14 moons so far.	
Conclusion New sub-heading.		Our solar system is an interesting phenomenon. We are continuing to explore space and there are many things we still do not know or understand about it. Our solar system is just one of thousands in our galaxy, The Milky Way. There are more than 100 billion galaxies in the universe that we know. Space is truly a deeply mysterious place.	Sub-heading or Paragraph Title – tells us what the paragraph is about and signals that we are coming to the end of the report. Present tense. Conclusion linking to introduction. It is okay if we do not know all the facts. Additional information to link back to introduction and conclude the report.

Discussion questions:

1. Where do you think we can find information about this topic?
2. What does the title tell us? Do you think it is important to have a title/ Why?
3. How do sub-headings help us?
4. What do you already know about our solar system?
5. Do the planets have different names in your home language?
6. List three things that the sun helps us with every day.

Model Text – Non-Annotated

Our Solar System
Introduction
Our solar system is the collection of planets, moons, asteroids, and comets that orbit around the Sun. It is about 4.6 billion years old and located in the Milky Way galaxy. Although space is extremely large and we do not know everything about it, we have a lot information about our solar system.

The Sun
The sun is the largest object in the centre of our solar system. However, the sun is not a planet. It is a star that is very bright and hot. All the planets orbit around the sun. It takes about 8 minutes for the light from the sun to reach earth. The light and heat from the sun allow things to live, grow, and survive on planet Earth. Without the sun, there will be no life on our planet.

Another important role the sun plays is to keep all the planets, asteroids, comets, and other rocks floating in space from crashing into each other. As the biggest object in our solar system, the sun's gravity makes sure that everything stays in its own orbit.

The Planets
There are eight planets in the solar system. They are Mercury, Venus, Earth, Mars, Jupiter, Saturn, Uranus, and Neptune. Pluto was once considered the ninth planet, but it was changed to a dwarf planet in 2006. All the planets move around the sun. The table below shows how the planets are different from each other:

Mercury	<ul><li>Closest to the sun.</li><li>The smallest planet in the solar system.</li><li>Does not have a moon.</li><li>The side facing the sun is very hot (426.7 degrees Celsius).</li><li>The side away from the sun is very cold (-173 degrees Celsius)</li><li>Does not have an atmosphere.</li></ul>
Venus	<ul><li>Second planet from the sun.</li><li>A little smaller than earth.</li><li>The hottest planet because it has a very thick atmosphere.</li><li>Too hot for life.</li><li>Does not have a moon.</li></ul>
Earth	<ul><li>We live here!</li><li>Third planet from the sun.</li><li>The only planet we know that has water on 71% of its surface.</li><li>Has one moon.</li><li>Takes 365 days to rotate around the sun.</li><li>Atmosphere has the perfect ingredients – 78% nitrogen, 21% oxygen, 1% other gasses – allows us to breathe.</li></ul>

| Mars | - Fourth planet from the sun.
- It is called the red planet because of iron on its surface.
- Has large volcanoes and deep valleys.
- We think that there may be water on Mars.
- Colder than earth. |
|---|---|
| Jupiter | - Fifth planet from the sun.
- Largest planet in the solar system.
- Has 63 moons so far.
- It is made up of gasses. |
| Saturn | - Sixth planet from the sun.
- Has a ring around it.
- It is the second largest planet in our solar system.
- Has 82 moons so far.
- It is a very cold planet. |
| Uranus | - Seventh planet from the sun.
- A cold planet – we call it an ice giant.
- Four times bigger than earth.
- Has 27 moons so far. |
| Neptune | - Eighth planet from the sun.
- It is called the blue planet.
- The furthest away from the sun.
- Very cold planet.
- It has 14 moons so far. |

Conclusion

Our solar system is an interesting phenomenon. We are continuing to explore space and there are many things we still do not know or understand about it. Our solar system is just one of thousands in our galaxy, The Milky Way. There are more than 100 billion galaxies in the universe that we know. Space is truly a deeply mysterious place.

Reading and Viewing Activities
A: Word Level

1. List all the verbs you can see.

2. The verbs are written in the _____ tense because _____.
3. Why do you think we use the word 'the' and capital letters when we write about our Solar System?
4. Why do we use "the" for sun, and planets?

5. List THREE words or phrases that tell you the facts of this topic may change in the future. Give a reason why you think so. One example has been done for you.

Word/phrase from the passage	My reason
"we do not know everything about it"	This tells me that we are still learning new things about space.

6. Why do you think we use " " (quotation marks) when we copy words or phrases from the passage?
   _____

7. List ONE new word you learnt from each sub-heading. What does it mean? Write your own sentence using the new word.

Paragraph	New word	Meaning	Write your own sentence using the word.
1			
2			
3			
4			

8. What did you do to find the meaning of new words?
   _____

9. What do these numbers tell us? What do we understand from this? The first one has been done for you.

Number	What it tells us	What I understand from this
4.6 billion	the age of solar system	Our solar system is very old.
8 minutes		
2006		
-173 degree		
71%		
365		

B: Sentence Level

Answer the questions using complete sentences.

1. Why do we need an introduction?
   _____

2. What is this descriptive report about?
   _____

3. List three sentences from the passage that tell you our solar system is a phenomenon.
   a. _____
   b. _____
   c. _____

4. Look at the beginning of the second paragraph of the sub-heading, "The Sun". What does the phrase "another important role" tells us about the sun?
   _____

5. List TWO interesting facts about each planet. One example has been done for you.

Neptune	
Saturn	
Mars	
Venus	
Mercury	-It is the closest planet to the sun. -It does not have a moon.
Earth	
Jupiter	
Uranus	

Write your own beginning sentence for each these sub-headings.

Sub-heading	Sentence from the passage	My own sentence
1 - Introduction	Our solar system is the collection of planets, moons, asteroids, and comets that orbit around the Sun.	
2 - The Sun	The sun is the largest object in the centre of our solar system.	
3 - The Planets	There are eight planets in the solar system.	
4 - Conclusion	Our solar system is an interesting phenomenon.	

C: Text Level

Write TWO sentences to show what each sub-heading is about. Then answer the two questions.

Sub-heading 1	
Sub-heading 2	
Sub-heading 3	
Sub-heading 4	
Think about how the writer has written about different things under each sub-heading. a. How does each sub-heading and the information under that connect to the title? b. How will you use this idea in your own writing?	a. b.

Functional Grammar

	Describe	What?	Extra Information
our	amazing	Solar System	is part of the universe.
		sun	
		planets	
		moon	
		days	
		volcanoes	
		earth	

D: Writing

Choose ONE planet OR the sun. Write your own Descriptive Report about it. Use the sub-headings to help you plan.

Title	
Introduction - What is _____? - What do we know about it?	
Name of the planet. What is it? Where in the solar system? What do we know about it? Can there be life on it? Why do you think so?	
3 Interesting facts about _____	
Conclusion	

Part Three – Intermediate/Developing Level – Descriptive Report

Genre 2, Text 2

Teacher's Notes: What is a Descriptive Report?

A descriptive report provides a detailed and objective description of a person, place, object, event, or phenomenon. The purpose of a descriptive report is to give the reader a clear and comprehensive understanding of the subject being described.

For English as an Additional Language/Dialect (EAL/D) students, descriptive reports can be a valuable tool for developing contextual and analytical skills, as well as for communicating scientific information in a clear and accessible way. They are an effective way to build objective research and academic writing skills.

Features of a Descriptive Report

- Accurate and factual – based on reliable sources.
- Clearly and logically organised – may include heading, sub-headings, images with captions, conclusion etc.
- Objective language – more facts, less personal opinions.
- Language features – e.g., adjectives and adverbs to create more depth.
- Contextualised - provide context of events, processes, objects being described.

Text 2 – Descriptive Report

Human Respiratory System

Researching and reporting about the Human Respiratory Systems allows students to connect with their own bodily functions. It is a starting point for further investigation on what happens within the human anatomy. This will help set them up for future descriptive report writing and is an example of how we can teach English using cross-curricular subject areas. Writing simple descriptive reports at the intermediate level allows students to experiment with fundamental skills for academic research and non-fiction work.

Part Three, Genre 2 – Descriptive Report
Human Respiratory System

Word Bank

respiratory	breathing
organs	important body parts inside the body – heart, liver, kidneys
tissues	our body is made of this
inhale	breathe in
exhale	breathe out
exchange	take something and give something
combine	mix together
contracts	gets smaller
expelled	let out
mucus membrane	a lining of slippery slime inside our bodies
monitors	checks
factors	reasons
nutrition	food that is healthy for us

Model Text – Annotated for whole class discussion

Structure	Descriptive Report	Language Features
Title	Human Respiratory System	Title – tells us what we are describing
Introduction We are introducing the topic.	Human beings breathe through their lungs. The human respiratory system is made up of several organs and tissues that work together to help us breathe. Breathing allows us to provide our body oxygen when we inhale and remove carbon dioxide when we exhale. When oxygen enters our lungs, they help us to exchange the gasses through our bloodstream. We call this process respiration which helps our organs and tissues receive oxygen and remove carbon dioxide. This exchange of gasses happens at the same time. The human respiratory system includes the nasal cavity (nose), oral cavity (mouth), pharynx (throat), larynx (voice box), trachea (windpipe), and lungs. RESPIRATORY SYSTEM [diagram with labels: Nasal Cavity, Oral Cavity, Larynx, Trachea, Right Lung, Left Lung, Bronchus, Bronchiole, Alveoli, LUNGS]	Sub-heading or Paragraph Title – tells us what the paragraph is about. The first two sentences introduce the reader to the topic. Present tense. Giving additional details about human breathing. Links to the title. Special science vocabulary – this is followed by a diagram with labels to help us "see" what we are describing.
Inhalation and Exhalation We are going into a new sub-heading	During inhalation or breathing in, air enters our body through our nose or mouth. It then passes through the pharynx, larynx, and trachea, which lead to the lungs. Within the lungs, the bronchi divide into smaller tubes called bronchioles, which end in small sacs called alveoli. The lungs then combine the oxygen with our blood so it can travel to all other body parts. Our body needs oxygen to break down food and create energy. Carbon dioxide from the bloodstream enters into the alveoli to be exhaled. Exhalation goes backwards through the same paths air entered our lungs.	Sub-heading or Paragraph Title – tells us what the paragraph is about. Linked to the sub-heading. Present tense. More information about the sub-heading. Links back to the introduction.
The Diaphragm New sub-heading	The diaphragm, a large muscle located at the bottom of the chest, plays an important role in breathing. When the diaphragm contracts, it pulls downward, causing air to enter the lungs. When the diaphragm relaxes, it pushes upward, causing air to be expelled from the lungs.	Sub-heading or Paragraph Title – tells us what the paragraph is about. Present tense. Linked to the sub-heading. More information about the sub-heading.
Interesting Facts New sub-heading	1. Adults breathe about 15 times per minute but newborn babies breathe about 60 times! 2. When our brain senses there is less oxygen in our body, it makes us yawn.	Sub-heading or Paragraph Title – tells us what the paragraph is about.

	3. Our left lung is smaller because our heart is next to it.	Present tense. Numbered for easy reading. Exclamation mark – tells us this is very interesting.
Additional Information New sub-heading.	Our respiratory system also includes interesting structures such as the nose, sinuses, and mucus membranes. They help to filter, warm, and moisten the air before it reaches the lungs. The system is controlled by the brain, which monitors the levels of oxygen and carbon dioxide in the bloodstream and adjusts our breathing rate accordingly. Various factors can affect respiratory health, such as smoking, air pollution, respiratory infections, and chronic respiratory diseases like asthma. It is important to maintain a healthy respiratory system through regular exercise and proper nutrition.	Sub-heading or Paragraph Title – tells us what the paragraph is about and signals that we are coming to the end of the report. Present tense. Linking to introduction. Additional facts linked to the topic. Adding some lifestyle factors that can affect the topic as part of the conclusion.

Discussion questions:
1. Where do you think we can find information about this topic?
2. What does the title tell us? Do you think it is important to have a title/ Why?
3. How do sub-headings help us?
4. What do you already know about the human respiratory system?
5. Do you think that the human body is clever?
6. List three things that can help us keep our lungs healthy.

Model Text – Non-Annotated

Human Respiratory System

Introduction

Human beings breathe through their lungs. The human respiratory system is made up of several organs and tissues that work together to help us breathe. Breathing allows us to provide our body oxygen when we inhale and remove carbon dioxide when we exhale. When oxygen enters our lungs, they help us to exchange the gasses through our bloodstream. We call this process respiration which helps our organs and tissues receive oxygen and remove carbon dioxide. This exchange of gasses happens at the same time.

The human respiratory system includes the nasal cavity (nose), oral cavity (mouth), pharynx (throat), larynx (voice box), trachea (windpipe), and lungs.

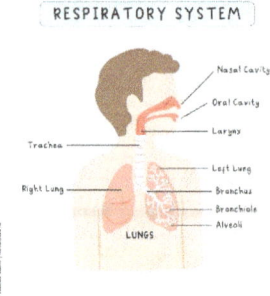

Inhalation and Exhalation

During inhalation or breathing in, air enters our body through our nose or mouth. It then passes through the pharynx, larynx, and trachea, which lead to the lungs. Within the lungs, the bronchi divide into smaller tubes called bronchioles, which end in small sacs called alveoli. The lungs then combine the oxygen with our blood so it can travel to all other body parts. Our body needs oxygen to break down food and create energy. Carbon dioxide from the bloodstream enters into the alveoli to be exhaled. Exhalation goes backwards through the same paths air entered our lungs.

The Diaphragm

The diaphragm, a large muscle located at the bottom of the chest, plays an important role in breathing. When the diaphragm contracts, it pulls downward, causing air to enter the lungs. When the diaphragm relaxes, it pushes upward, causing air to be expelled from the lungs.

Interesting Facts

1. Adults breathe about 15 times per minute but newborn babies breathe about 60 times!
2. When our brain senses there is less oxygen in our body, it makes us yawn.
3. Our left lung is smaller because our heart is next to it.

Additional Information

Our respiratory system also includes interesting structures such as the nose, sinuses, and mucus membranes. They help to filter, warm, and moisten the air before it reaches the lungs. The system is controlled by the brain, which monitors the levels of oxygen and carbon dioxide in the bloodstream and adjusts our breathing rate accordingly.

Various factors can affect respiratory health, such as smoking, air pollution, respiratory infections, and chronic respiratory diseases like asthma. It is important to maintain a healthy respiratory system through regular exercise and proper nutrition.

Reading and Viewing Activities

A: Word Level

1. List all the verbs you can see.

   [   ]

2. The verbs are written in the _____ tense because _____.
3. Why do you think we use the word "human" in this topic?
4. What does the word "organs" mean in this passage? Do you know any other meaning of this word?
5. List THREE words that tell you this is a science topic. Give a reason why you think so. One example has been done for you.

Word/phrase from the passage	My reason
"nasal cavity"	This tells me that we are a science word for nose.

6. Explain the words below.

Breathing	
Respiration	

7. List ONE new word you learnt from each sub-heading. What does it mean? Write your own sentence using the new word.

Paragraph	New word	Meaning	Write your own sentence using the word.
1			
2			
3			
4			
5			

8. What did you do to find the meaning of new words?
   _____

9. What do these words tell us? What do we understand from this? The first one has been done for you.

Word	What it tells us	What I understand from this
system	Many things are happening	The human body does many things to breathe.
provide		
process		
role		
monitors		
affect		

B: Sentence Level

Answer the questions using complete sentences.

1. Why do we need an introduction?
   _____

2. What is this descriptive report about?
   _____

3. List three sentences from the passage that tell you our respiratory system is a complex process.
   a. _____
   b. _____
   c. _____

4. Look at last line in under the first sub-heading. Why are there words written in brackets? How do they help you?
   _____

5. List ONE interesting fact about each word below. One example has been done for you.

lungs	
nose	Help to filter the air we breathe.
newborn babies	
brain	
oxygen	

Write your own beginning sentence for each these sub-headings.

Sub-heading	Sentence from the passage	My own sentence
Introduction	Human beings breathe through their lungs.	
Inhalation and Exhalation	During inhalation or breathing in, air enters our body through our nose or mouth.	
The Diaphragm	The diaphragm, a large muscle located at the bottom of the chest, plays an important role in breathing.	
Additional Information	Our respiratory system also includes interesting structures such as the nose, sinuses, and mucus membranes.	

C: Text Level

Write TWO sentences to show what each sub-heading is about. Then answer the two questions.

Sub-heading 1	
Sub-heading 2	
Sub-heading 3	
Sub-heading 4	
Sub-heading 5	

Think about how the writer has written about different things under each sub-heading. a. How does each sub-heading and the information under that connect to the title? b. How will you use this idea in your own writing?	a. b.

Functional Grammar

	Describe	What?	Extra Information
our	amazing	lungs	help us breathe.
		gasses	
		nose	
		larynx	
		tubes	
		air	
		exercise	

D: Writing

Find out about the Human Digestive System. Write your own Descriptive Report about it. Use the sub-headings to help you plan.

Title	
Introduction - What is _____? - What do we know about it? - Labelled diagram	
How does our food travel from the mouth to the stomach?	
What happens in the stomach?	
3 Interesting facts about the human digestive system.	
Additional Information	

Unlocking Genre

Part Three – Intermediate/Developing Level – Book Report

Genre 3, Text 1

Teacher's Notes: What is a Book Report?

A book report summarises and evaluates a book or other literary work. The purpose of a book report is to give the reader a brief overview of the book's content and to provide a critical analysis of its strengths and weaknesses.

Book reports can take many forms, such as summaries, reviews, and analyses. They often include information about the author, the plot, the setting, the characters, and the themes or messages of the book. When writing a book report, it is important to read the book carefully and take notes on important information and details.

For English as an Additional Language/Dialect (EAL/D) students, book reports can be a valuable tool for developing critical thinking and analytical skills, as well as for clearly and effectively communicating their personal opinions. They are an effective way to build a positive relationship with reading for pleasure and an appreciation of various types of literature.

Features of a Book Report

- Introduction to the book – title, author, background information, genre, etc.
- Summary – plot, main themes.
- Analysis – strengths and weaknesses – reviewer's opinion, characters, plot, themes.
- Subjective language – personal opinions.
- Language features – e.g., adjectives and adverbs to create more depth.
- Conclusion – summary of main points, final evaluation/recommendation

Text 1 – Book Report

The Little Refugee

Reading and reporting on a book allows EAL/D students to build confidence in sharing their personal opinions. It is a starting point to enhance their reading skills and grow a love for reading. This will help set them up for future text analysis writing and is an example of how we can teach complex language skills using more manageable texts. Writing simple book reports at the intermediate level allows students to experiment with fundamental skills for critical text analysis.

Part Three, Genre 3 – Book Report
The Little Refugee by Ahn Doh

Word Bank

first person	using I, we, us, me, mine, ours, myself, ourselves
illustrated	the book has pictures and drawings done by someone
autobiography	writing about our own life story
extraordinary	amazing
unusual	not normal
experiences	things that happened to someone
struggles	problems they faced
new environment	new place
vibrant colours	bright colours
imagine	see in our mind
resilience	being strong
determination	not giving up
important values	important beliefs
heart-warming	makes the reader happy
inspiring	making the reader feel that they also can do something good
challenges	difficult situations

Model Text – Annotated for whole class discussion

Structure	Book Report	Language Features
Title	Book Report The Little Refugee By Ahn Do and Suzanne Do (2011) Illustrated by Bruce Whatley	Title Author/s and Year Published Illustrator
Introduction We are introducing the book with some basic information.	*The Little Refugee* is written in the first person by Ahn Do and his wife Suzanne Do. It is a picture book illustrated by Bruce Whatley. The book is an autobiography of Ahn Do's extraordinary and sometimes scary journey from Vietnam to his life in Australia.	Title of book is in *italics* when typing. When writing, you need to underline the title. Present tense Tells you which pronoun the author is using. What type of book. Acknowledging the artist. What the book is about.
Summary We are providing a short summary about the book.	The book starts with Ahn Do's life in Vietnam. He calls it "a crazy place" that has unusual food and traffic laws. His family was very poor and most of the family lived together in a small house but Ahn Do was happy playing with all the children. Unfortunately, there was a war and Ahn Do's father fought in it along with American and Australian soldiers. So, Ahn Do's family had to leave after it ended as it was dangerous for his father to continue living in Vietnam.	How does the book begin? Present tense. Quote from the book. Past tense – discussing the past. Summarises the past and the reason for the author's journey. Adverb – tells us that something sad or bad is about to happen.
Analysis Gives us some details about the story and the book.	Ahn Do writes about how his family's journey to Australia in a small fishing boat was full of danger and frightening experiences. He then tells the reader about his new life and all the new experiences of going to school and growing up in Australia. He also talks about his parents' struggles and hard work while trying to fit into a new environment. The book is beautifully illustrated, with vibrant colours and detailed drawings that help us imagine Ahn Do's life and journey. *The Little Refugee* shows us that resilience and determination to succeed are important values of refugees. Ahn Do also discusses the importance of family and community support when settling into a new country. Above all, he shows us that education and following our dreams help us to be successful and happy.	Present tense Some details about what the author's life and message that can be found in the book. Linking/transition words – help the analysis to flow. Personal opinions about the book.
Conclusion Summarises the book report. Gives personal recommendation.	Overall, *The Little Refugee* is a heart-warming and inspiring story that shows us the experiences of refugees and the challenges they face. I recommend this book because although many difficult things happened in Ahn Do's life, he managed to work hard and find happiness. This is something we can all try to achieve.	Tells us that we are ending our report. Personal opinion. Recommendation.

Discussion questions:
1. What does the title tell us? Do you think it is important to have a title/ Why?
2. What do we need to do BEFORE we write a book report?
3. How do sub-headings help us?
4. What do you already know about Ahn Do?
5. What is your story?
6. List three things that make you want to read this book.

Model Text – Non-Annotated

Book Report

The Little Refugee
By Ahn Do and Suzanne Do (2011)
Illustrated by Bruce Whatley

Introduction
The Little Refugee is written in the first person by Ahn Do and his wife Suzanne Do. It is a picture book illustrated by Bruce Whatley. The book is an autobiography of Ahn Do's extraordinary and sometimes scary journey from Vietnam to his life in Australia.

Summary
The book starts with Ahn Do's life in Vietnam. He calls it "a crazy place" that has unusual food and traffic laws. His family was very poor and most of the family lived together in a small house but Ahn Do was happy playing with all the children.

Unfortunately, there was a war and Ahn Do's father fought in it along with American and Australian soldiers. So, Ahn Do's family had to leave after it ended as it was dangerous for his father to continue living in Vietnam.

Analysis
Ahn Do writes about how his family's journey to Australia in a small fishing boat was full of danger and frightening experiences. He then tells the reader about his new life and all the new experiences of going to school and growing up in Australia. He also talks about his parents' struggles and hard work while trying to fit into a new environment.

The book is beautifully illustrated, with vibrant colours and detailed drawings that help us imagine Ahn Do's life and journey. The Little Refugee shows us that resilience and determination to succeed are important values of refugees. Ahn Do also discusses the importance of family and community support when settling into a new country. Above all, he shows us that education and following our dreams help us to be successful and happy.

Conclusion
Overall, The Little Refugee is a heart-warming and inspiring story that shows us the experiences of refugees and the challenges they face. I recommend this book because although many difficult things happened in Ahn Do's life, he managed to work hard and find happiness. This is something we can all try to achieve.

Reading and Viewing Activities

A: Word Level

1. List all the verbs you can see.

2. Why do you think the verbs are sometimes in the present tense and sometimes in the past tense?

3. What information can you get from the highlighted words/numbers below?

By Ahn Do and Suzanne Do	
Illustrated by	
2011	

4. List THREE words that tell you this is a book report. Give a reason why you think so. One example has been done for you.

Word/phrase from the passage	My reason
"is written in the first person"	This tells me that someone wrote about their own life.

5. Explain the words below.

Picture book	
Autobiography	
Inspiring story	

6. List TWO new words you learnt from each sub-heading. What do they mean? Write your own sentence using the new word.

Paragraph	New words	Meaning	Write your own sentence using the word.
1			
2			
3			
4			

7. What did you do to find the meaning of new words?

8. What do these headings tell us? What do we understand from this? The first one has been done for you.

Word	What it tells us	What I understand from this
Introduction	The reader is given some information about the book.	I know what the book is going to be about.
Summary		
Analysis		
Conclusion		

Unlocking Genre

B: Sentence Level

Answer the questions using complete sentences.

1. Why do we need an introduction?
   _____

2. What is this book report about?
   _____

3. List three sentences from the passage that tell you Ahn Do had a difficult journey when his family travelled from Vietnam to Australia.
   a. _____
   b. _____
   c. _____

4. Does this book report recommend that we should read this book? How do you know this?
   _____

5. What can we guess from the words/phrases below? One example has been done for you.

first person	
unusual food	
small fishing boat	The journey was dangerous because a small fishing boat can drown easily in a storm.
his parents' struggles	
detailed drawings	
I recommend this book	

Write your own beginning sentence for each these sub-headings.

Sub-heading	Sentence from the passage	My own sentence
Introduction	*The Little Refugee* is written in the first person by Ahn Do and his wife Suzanne Do.	
Summary	The book starts with Ahn Do's life in Vietnam.	
Analysis	Ahn Do writes about how his family's journey to Australia in a small fishing boat was full of danger and frightening experiences.	
Conclusion	Overall, *The Little Refugee* is a heart-warming and inspiring story that shows us the experiences of refugees and the challenges they face.	

C: Text Level

Write TWO sentences to show what each sub-heading is about. Then answer the two questions.

Sub-heading 1	
Sub-heading 2	
Sub-heading 3	
Sub-heading 4	
Think about how the writer has written about different things under each sub-heading. a. How does each sub-heading and the information under that connect to the title? b. How will you use this idea in your own writing?	a. b.

Functional Grammar

	Describe	What?	Extra Information
a	picture	book	with beautiful drawings.
		place	
		food	
		house	
		children	
		boat	
		school	
		colours	
		story	

D: Writing

Complete reading a book. Write your own Book Report about it. Use the sub-headings and questions to help you plan.

Title	Book Report
Author/s Illustrator/s	
Introduction	• Written in 1st or 3rd person • What type of book? – picture book, short stories, children's book etc.
Summary	• What is it about? • How does it start? • What happened?
Analysis	• Is it well written/ • Is it easy to read/understand? • Are there pictures/drawings? – what do they do to help the reader? • What can we learn from this book?
Conclusion	• Recommendation – yes/no? Why?

Part Three – Intermediate/Developing Level – Book Report

Genre 3, Text 2

Teacher's Notes: What is a Book Report?

A book report summarises and evaluates a book or other literary work. The purpose of a book report is to give the reader a brief overview of the book's content and to provide a critical analysis of its strengths and weaknesses.

Book reports can take many forms, such as summaries, reviews, and analyses. They often include information about the author, the plot, the setting, the characters, and the themes or messages of the book. When writing a book report, it is important to read the book carefully and take notes on important information and details.

For English as an Additional Language/Dialect (EAL/D) students, book reports can be a valuable tool for developing critical thinking and analytical skills, as well as for clearly and effectively communicating their personal opinions. They are an effective way to build a positive relationship with reading for pleasure and an appreciation of various types of literature.

Features of a Book Report

- Introduction to the book – title, author, background information, genre, etc.
- Summary – plot, main themes.
- Analysis – strengths and weaknesses – reviewer's opinion, characters, plot, themes.
- Subjective language – personal opinions.
- Language features – e.g., adjectives and adverbs to create more depth.
- Conclusion – summary of main points, final evaluation/recommendation

Text 2 – Book Report

The Rabbits

Reading and reporting on a book allows EAL/D students to build confidence in sharing their personal opinions. It is a starting point to enhance their reading skills and grow a love for reading. This will help set them up for future text analysis writing and is an example of how we can teach complex language skills using more manageable texts. Writing simple book reports at the intermediate level allows students to experiment with fundamental skills for critical text analysis.

Part Three, Genre 3 – Book Report
The Rabbits by John Marsden and Shaun Tan

Word Bank

third person	using they, them
illustrated	the book has pictures and drawings done by someone
colonisation	taking over and settling down in a new country by using force.
invasion	attacking and taking what belongs to someone else.
depict	describe
consequences	things that happened because of the invasion.
allegory	a word that hides the real meaning.
stolen generation	Aboriginal children who were taken away from their families by the colonisers.
symbolised	a word that means something else.
erase	remove or rub away
confusion	not sure about something.
marsupials	mammals that have pouches to carry their babies.
vibrant	bright colours
issues	problems
trauma	an experience that makes a person very sad and scared.
beneficial	good

Model Text – Annotated for whole class discussion

Structure	Book Report	Language Features
Title	Book Report The Rabbits By John Marsden (1998) Illustrated by Shaun Tan	Title Author/s and Year Published Illustrator
Introduction We are introducing the book with some basic information.	*The Rabbits* is written in the third person by John Marsden. It is a picture book illustrated by Shaun Tan. The book uses rabbits as a way of telling the story of the British colonisation of Australia. It is also a story of the environmental damage caused by this invasion. It has only two or three sentences on each page. The storytelling is done more through the pictures painted by Shaun Tan to depict the issues, feelings, and consequences of the arrival of the British on Australian soil.	Title of book is in *italics* when typing. When writing, you need to underline the title. Present tense Tells you which pronoun the author is using. What type of book. Acknowledging the artist. What the book is about.
Summary We are providing a short summary about the book.	The book starts with the sentence, "The Rabbits came many grandparents ago". This tells us that it is about an event that happened long ago. The word "came" shows that "rabbits" is an allegory about people as they "came" on their own. Through the pictures and sentences, we are taken on a journey of invasion, sadness, misunderstanding of local beliefs and cultures, environmental damage, and the stolen generation.	How does the book begin? Present tense. Quote from the book. Using one word to mean something else. Summarises the events that made the author write this book. A list of events to come.
Analysis Gives us some details about the story and the book.	John Marsden writes about how the arrival of the British, symbolised in this book as rabbits, slowly began to erase the local cultures of the Aboriginal people, represented by kangaroos and wombats. He tells the reader how this arrival "by water" created confusion and worry amongst the people who were already living in Australia. The colonisers brought new ways of living, unfamiliar food, and animals into the space. They spread all over the new country and this caused small wars between the marsupials and the rabbits. As there were more rabbits than kangaroos and wombats, the rabbits won the war. They continued to take what they wanted from the land. This caused many problems for the environment. They also took the children away from the local people. The book ends with all that has been lost and with hope that someone would save the marsupials from the rabbits.	Present tense Past Tense – telling us what happened in the past. Some details about what the book is about: Personal opinions about the book. Linking words to allow flow.

	The book is beautifully illustrated, with vibrant full-page paintings that show us some of the terrible things that happened after the British arrived in Australia. Shaun Tan uses bright and dark colours to show the different issues and emotions discussed throughout the book. Although there are less words and more pictures, this book helps us understand the suffering, pain, and trauma that the Aboriginal people experienced due to colonisation. We are left with the thought that this suffering is still ongoing today.	
Conclusion Summarises the book report. Gives personal recommendation.	Overall, *The Rabbits* is a serious book that tells us about how the changes brought by colonisation are not always beneficial to the people who already live in a place. As the book does not actually use the word Australia, we can say that it also represents the problems caused by colonisation to Aboriginal people around the world. It is a good book to read as it gives the reader a historical recount of shocking events in an easy-to-read picture book.	Tells us that we are ending our report. Personal opinion. Recommendation.

Discussion questions:

1. What does the title tell us? Do you think it is important to have a title/ Why?
2. What do we need to do BEFORE we write a book report?
3. How do sub-headings help us?
4. What do you already know about colonisation?
5. Was your home country colonised? If yes, by which country? What did they do?
6. List three things that make you want to read this book.

Model Text – Non-Annotated

Book report

The Rabbits
By John Marsden (1998)
Illustrated by Shaun Tan
Introduction

The Rabbits is written in the third person by John Marsden. It is a picture book illustrated by Shaun Tan. The book is uses rabbits as a way of telling the story of the British colonisation of Australia. It is also a story of the environmental damage caused by this invasion. It has only two or three sentences on each page. The storytelling is done more through the pictures painted by Shaun Tan to depict the issues, feelings, and consequences of the arrival of the British on Australian soil.

Summary
The book starts with the sentence, "The Rabbits came many grandparents ago". This tells us that it is about an event that happened long ago. The word "came" shows that "rabbits" is an allegory about people as they "came" on their own. Through the pictures and sentences, we are taken on a journey of invasion, sadness, misunderstanding of local beliefs and cultures, environmental damage, and the stolen generation.

Analysis

John Marsden writes about how the arrival of the British, symbolised in this book as rabbits, slowly began to erase the local cultures of the Aboriginal people, represented by kangaroos and wombats. He tells the reader how this arrival "by water" created confusion and worry amongst the people who were already living in Australia. The colonisers brought new ways of living, unfamiliar food, and animals into the space. They spread all over the new country and this caused small wars between the marsupials and the rabbits.

As there were more rabbits than kangaroos and wombats, the rabbits won the war. They continued to take what they wanted from the land. This caused many problems for the environment. They also took the children away from the local people. The book ends with all that has been lost and with hope that someone would save the marsupials from the rabbits.

The book is beautifully illustrated, with vibrant full-page paintings that show us some of the terrible things that happened after the British arrived in Australia. Shaun Tan uses bright and dark colours to show the different issues and emotions discussed throughout the book. Although there are less words and more pictures, this book helps us understand the suffering, pain, and trauma that the Aboriginal people experienced due to colonisation. We are left with the thought that this suffering is still ongoing today.

Conclusion

Overall, *The Rabbits* is a serious book that tells us about how the changes brought by colonisation are not always beneficial to the people who already live in a place. As the book does not actually use the word Australia, we can say that it also represents the problems caused by colonisation to Aboriginal people around the world. It is a good book to read as it gives the reader a historical recount of shocking events in an easy-to-read picture book.

Reading and Viewing Activities

A: Word Level

1. List all the verbs you can see.

2. Why do you think the verbs are sometimes in the present tense and sometimes in the past tense?

3. What information can you get from the highlighted words/numbers below?

By John Marsden	
Illustrated by	
1998	

4. List THREE words that tell you this is a book report. Give a reason why you think so. One example has been done for you.

Word/phrase from the passage	My reason
"is written in the third person"	This tells me that this book is about someone else and not about the writer.

5. Explain the words/phrases below.

Picture book	
Allegory	
Arrival by water	

6. List TWO new words you learnt from each sub-heading. What do they mean? Write your own sentence using the new word.

Paragraph	New words	Meaning	Write your own sentence using the word.
1			
2			
3			
4			

7. What did you do to find the meaning of new words?
_____

8. What do these headings tell us? What do we understand from this? The first one has been done for you.

Word	What it tells us	What I understand from this
Introduction	The reader is given some information about the book.	I know what the book is going to be about.
Summary		
Analysis		
Conclusion		

B: Sentence Level

Answer the questions using complete sentences.

1. Why do we need an introduction?
_____

2. What is this book report about?
_____

3. List three sentences from the passage that tell you Aboriginal people were not happy with the colonisers.
   a. _____
   b. _____
   c. _____

4. Does this book report recommend that we should read this book? How do you know this?
_____

5. What can we guess from the words/phrases below? One example has been done for you.

third person	
invasion	Taking something by force.
many grandparents ago	
symbolised	
vibrant paintings	
pain and trauma	

Unlocking Genre 142

Write your own beginning sentence for each these sub-headings.

Sub-heading	Sentence from the passage	My own sentence
Introduction	*The Rabbits* is written in the third person by John Marsden.	
Summary	The book starts with the sentence, "The Rabbits came many grandparents ago".	
Analysis – Paragraph 1	John Marsden writes about how the arrival of the British, symbolised in this book as rabbits, slowly began to erase the local cultures of the Aboriginal people, represented by kangaroos and wombats.	
Analysis – Paragraph 2	As there were more rabbits than kangaroos and wombats, the rabbits won the war.	
Analysis – Paragraph 3	The book is beautifully illustrated, with vibrant full-page paintings that show us some of the terrible things that happened after the British arrived in Australia.	
Conclusion	Overall, *The Rabbits* is a serious book that tells us about how the changes brought by colonisation are not always beneficial to the people who already live in a place.	

C: Text Level

Write TWO sentences to show what each sub-heading is about. Then answer the two questions.

Sub-heading 1	
Sub-heading 2	
Sub-heading 3	
Sub-heading 4	
Think about how the writer has written about different things under each sub-heading. a. How does each sub-heading and the information under that connect to the title? b. How will you use this idea in your own writing?	a. b.

Functional Grammar

	Describe	What?	Extra Information
the	angry	rabbits	won the war.
		environment	
		journey	
		cultures	
		marsupials	
		food	
		land	
		paintings	
		events	

D: Writing

Complete reading a book. Write your own Book Report about it. Use the sub-headings and questions to help you plan.

Title	Book Report
Author/s Illustrator/s	
Introduction	• Written in 1st or 3rd person • What type of book? – picture book, short stories, children's book etc.
Summary	• What is it about? • How does it start? • What happened?
Analysis	• Is it well written/ • Is it easy to read/understand? • Are there pictures/drawings? – what do they do to help the reader? • What can we learn from this book?
Conclusion	• Recommendation – yes/no? Why?

PART FOUR:
English as an Additional Language/Dialect (EAL/D) – Advanced/Consolidating Level

Who Are Advanced/Consolidating EAL/D Students?

Advanced/Consolidating EAL/D students are developing a higher level of proficiency in the English language and are working towards achieving near-native fluency. They are considered as competent in a wider range of social and academic contexts.

Challenges Faced by Advanced/Consolidating EAL/D Students

While advanced/consolidating EAL/D students are near native user proficiency, they still encounter challenges within the complex nuances of the English language:

- Idiomatic Expressions: Mastering the use of idiomatic expressions and colloquial language will still continue to challenge EAL/D students at this level.
- Academic Writing: Excelling in advanced academic writing, which may include research and various forms of presentations.
- Cultural Differences: Navigating cultural nuances and challenges that may come with that.

Strategies to Support Advanced/Consolidating EAL/D Students

To help advanced/consolidating EAL/D students on their quest for near-native fluency, consider the following strategies:

- Independent Research and Study: Foster the development of independent research and study skills.
- Advanced Academic Support: Provide guidance in advanced academic writing, research methodologies, and presentation skills.
- Study Skills: Explicitly teach and reinforce editing, note taking, and summarising skills.

Genres and some Australian Curriculum links for this level:

Genre	Topic	Australian Curriculum link
Science Report	Electricity – Conductors and Insulators	<ul><li>identifying and describing text structures and language features used in a variety of texts, including some literary texts (ACEEA193)</li><li>using common subject-specific vocabulary, synonyms, antonyms and collocations (ACEEA199)</li><li>using simple, compound and some complex sentences (ACEEA202)</li></ul>
	The Lifecycle of a Bean Plant	<ul><li>identifying and describing text structures and language features used in a variety of texts, including some literary texts (ACEEA193)</li><li>using common subject-specific vocabulary, synonyms, antonyms and collocations (ACEEA199)</li><li>using simple, compound and some complex sentences (ACEEA202)</li></ul>
Text Analysis	Film – Moana	<ul><li>identifying and describing text structures and language features used in a variety of texts, including some literary texts (ACEEA193)</li><li>identifying and describing how cultural variations in values and beliefs, for example, respect or honour, and the concepts of community and society, are represented by language. (ACEEA196)</li><li>using strategies for planning and refining work such as editing for consistent use of common punctuation. (ACEEA204)</li><li>using simple, compound and some complex sentences (ACEEA202)</li></ul>

	Poem – The Road Not Taken	<ul><li>identifying and describing text structures and language features used in a variety of texts, including some literary texts (ACEEA193)</li><li>using imaginative and descriptive language and growing control over direct and indirect speech (ACEEA200)</li><li>using strategies for planning and refining work such as editing for consistent use of common punctuation. (ACEEA204)</li><li>using simple, compound and some complex sentences (ACEEA202)</li></ul>
Language Analysis	Blog – Climate Change	<ul><li>identifying and describing text structures and language features used in a variety of texts, including some literary texts (ACEEA193)</li><li>explaining how meaning changes with shifts in tone and register (ACEEA195)</li><li>using appropriate form, content and style for a range of common, and some unfamiliar, purposes and audiences (ACEEA197)</li><li>using strategies for planning and refining work such as editing for consistent use of common punctuation. (ACEEA204)</li><li>using simple, compound and some complex sentences (ACEEA202)</li></ul>
	Letter to Editor	<ul><li>identifying and describing text structures and language features used in a variety of texts, including some literary texts (ACEEA193)</li><li>explaining how meaning changes with shifts in tone and register (ACEEA195)</li><li>using appropriate form, content and style for a range of common, and some unfamiliar, purposes and audiences (ACEEA197)</li><li>using strategies for planning and refining work such as editing for consistent use of common punctuation. (ACEEA204)</li><li>using simple, compound and some complex sentences (ACEEA202)</li></ul>

Genre 1, Text 1

Teacher's Notes: What is a Science Report?

A science report presents the results of scientific research or experimentation. The purpose of a science report is to communicate scientific findings and to provide a clear and accurate summary of the methods, results, and conclusions of the study.

Science reports can take many forms, such as lab reports, research papers, scientific articles, and technical reports. They often include a description of the research question or hypothesis, the methods used to conduct the study, the results of the study, and a discussion of the significance and implications of the findings.

When writing a science report, it is important to use clear and concise language, and to organise the information in a logical and coherent manner. The report should include a description of the procedures and techniques used in the study, as well as any data, graphs, or other visual aids that help to illustrate the findings.

For English as an Additional Language/Dialect (EAL/D) students, science reports can be a valuable tool for developing research and presentation skills, as well as for communicating scientific information in a clear and accessible way. They are an effective way to build objective research and academic writing skills.

Features of a Science Report

- Includes Title and Abstract/Summary of the investigation.
- Introduction – provides background information, research question, and hypothesis.
- Aim – explains why an experiment is being conducted.
- Hypothesis – what is the predicted result?
- Materials – a list of all the materials needed.
- Method – a step by step of what was done.
- Result – may include graphs, tables, diagrams, pictures etc.
- Discussion – what was found and what else could have happened?
- Conclusion – main findings, what that means, future possibilities, etc.
- Reference – articles, textbooks, etc.
- Accurate and factual – based on experiments/research.
- Clearly and logically organised – may include heading, sub-headings, images with captions, conclusion etc.
- Objective language – more facts, less personal opinions.
- Language features – metalanguage, technical terms, etc.

Text 1 – Science Report

Electricity – Conductors and Non-conductors

Writing a science report about Electricity allows students to connect with current climate change issues and research in sustainable use of resources. Writing a science report about conductors and non-conductors of electricity can help EAL/D students explore and discuss about existing and future possibilities of electricity use in our daily lives. This will help set them up for future science report writing and is an example of how we can teach English using cross-curricular subject areas. Writing simple science reports at the advanced level allows students to experiment with fundamental skills for academic research and non-fiction work.

Part Four, Genre 1 – Science Report
Electricity – Conductors and Insulators

Word Bank

devices	Things we use such as mobile phones, televisions, computers etc.
conductor	Something that allows electricity to flow through it.
insulator	Something that does not allow electricity to flow through it.
aim	The reason for the science experiment.
hypothesis	An idea that can be tested to see if it is true or false.
materials	Things needed for an experiment.
method	How the science experiment was conducted.
submerged	Completely covered by liquid.
warning	Something that we need to be careful of.

Model Text – Annotated for whole class discussion

Structure	Science Report	Language Features
Title Date	**Electricity – Conductors and Insulators** **Wednesday 18th October 2023**	Title – tells us what the experiment is about. Date – tells us when this experiment was conducted and helps us to compare with past or future similar experiments.
Introduction We are introducing the topic.	Electricity is an important part of our lives. Without electricity, we would not be able to use any of our devices such as our mobile phones, televisions, and tablets. Did you know that some things allow electricity to flow through them? They are called conductors. On the other hand, there are some things that do not allow electricity to flow through them. These are labelled as insulators. Knowing this is important and may save our lives.	Gives a little background about the experiment. Present tense.
Aim	The aim of this experiment is to test different materials to see if they conduct electricity.	• States the purpose of the experiment – just one or two sentences. • Present tense.
Hypothesis	Some materials are conductors of electricity and some materials are insulators.	• Prediction of the result – one or two sentences. • Present tense.
Materials	• Four crocodile clip wires • A circuit light bulb • A 9V battery • Piece of wood • An aluminium wire • A copper wire • A sheet of paper • A glass of water • A glass of cooking oil • A balloon • A plastic bottle • A metal spoon	• List of all the materials used in the experiment.
Method	1. Two crocodile clips (a and b) were attached to the two sides of the 9V battery. 2. One end of clip a was attached to the light bulb. 3. One end of clip b was used to attach the different materials. 4. One end of another crocodile clip (c) was attached to the bulb. 5. The other end of clip c was attached to the material. 6. Every time the bulb lit up the material used was added to the conductor pile 7. When the bulb did not light up, the material was added to the insulator pile.	• Step by step of what was done. • Sequential from first to last step. • Past tense • Warning – only if necessary.

Unlocking Genre 149

	8. For water and oil, the crocodile clips were submerged into the liquids. 9. The last material used was the hand of one of the team members. **(WARNING: This was done because the battery did not have enough power to harm a human. Please do not try this with electricity in your house!)**	
Diagram	*(hand-drawn diagram showing Clip b, Clip a, Crocodile Clips wire, Battery 9v, Light Bulb, Clip c, and Material)*	• Shows what happened in the experiment. • Labels tell us what materials were used. • The diagram can be drawn by hand as in this example.
Results						• Usually written in a table format. • Tells us what we saw and noted during the experiment.
	Material	Observation of light bulb	Conductor	Insulator	
	Wood	Light off		Yes	
	Aluminium Wire	Light on	Yes		
	Copper wire	Light on	Yes		
	Paper	Light off		Yes	
	Water	Light on	Yes		
	Oil	Light off		Yes	
	Balloon	Light off		Yes	
	Plastic bottle	Light off		Yes	
	Metal spoon	Light on	Yes		
	Human hand	Light on	Yes		
Discussion	Most metals were conductors of electricity and most non-metallic materials were insulators. Both types are important when we build electrical circuits in our homes and public spaces. Although water and oil are both liquids, water was a conductor and oil was an insulator. We were surprised to find out that our bodies were conductors of electricity. This means that we have to be careful when touching electrical things around us. Only metallic materials could have been tested to see if all metals conducted electricity. More materials could also have been added to the list.	• Reflecting on what happened during the experiment. • Thinking about what else we could have done. • Any new findings – only if it happens. • Past tense.
Conclusion	Some materials were conductors of electricity and some materials were insulators and do not allow electricity to flow through them.	• Short statement. • Linked to the aim. • Past tense.

Unlocking Genre

Discussion questions:
1. Where do you think this experiment took place?
2. What does the title tell us? Do you think it is important to have a title/ Why?
3. What does the date tell us? Why is this important in a science report?
4. How do the sub-headings help us?
5. What do you already know about science reports?
6. Think about a science experiment that you would like to conduct. What would you do first?
7. List three benefits of electricity.

Model Text – Non-Annotated

Electricity – Conductors and Insulators
Wednesday 18th October 2023

Introduction
Electricity is an important part of our lives. Without electricity, we would not be able to use any of our devices such as our mobile phones, televisions, and tablets. Did you know that some things allow electricity to flow through them? They are called conductors. On the other hand, there are some things that do not allow electricity to flow through them. These are labelled as insulators. Knowing this is important and may save our lives.

Aim
The aim of this experiment is to test different materials to see if they conduct electricity.

Hypothesis
Some materials are conductors of electricity and some materials are insulators.

Materials
- Four crocodile clip wires
- A circuit light bulb
- A 9V battery
- Piece of wood
- An aluminium wire
- A copper wire
- A sheet of paper
- A glass of water
- A glass of cooking oil
- A balloon
- A plastic bottle
- A metal spoon

Method
1. Two crocodile clips (a and b) were attached to the two sides of the 9V battery.
2. One end of clip a was attached to the light bulb.
3. One end of clip b was used to attach the different materials.
4. One end of another crocodile clip (c) was attached to the bulb.
5. The other end of clip c was attached to the material.
6. Every time the bulb lit up the material used was added to the conductor pile
7. When the bulb did not light up, the material was added to the insulator pile.
8. For water and oil, the crocodile clips were submerged into the liquids.
9. The last material used was the hand of one of the team members. (WARNING: This was done because the battery did not have enough power to harm a human. Please do not try this with electricity in your house!)

Diagram

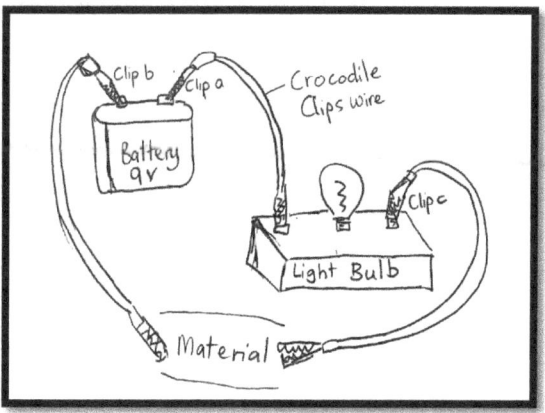

Results

Material	Observation of light bulb	Conductor	Insulator
Wood	Light off		Yes
Aluminium Wire	Light on	Yes	
Copper wire	Light on	Yes	
Paper	Light off		Yes
Water	Light on	Yes	
Oil	Light off		Yes
Balloon	Light off		Yes
Plastic bottle	Light off		Yes
Metal spoon	Light on	Yes	
Human hand	Light on	Yes	

Discussion

Most metals were conductors of electricity and most non-metallic materials were insulators. Both types are important when we build electrical circuits in our homes and public spaces. Although water and oil are both liquids, water was a conductor and oil was an insulator. We were surprised to find out that our bodies were conductors of electricity. This means that we have to be careful when touching electrical things around us. Only metallic materials could have been tested to see if all metals conducted electricity. More materials could also have been added to the list.

Conclusion

Some materials were conductors of electricity and some materials were insulators and do not allow electricity to flow through them.

Reading and Viewing Activities

A: Word Level

1. List all the verbs you can see.

   [   ]

2. The verbs are written in the _____ tense because _____.
3. What do the words 'conductors' and 'insulators' mean?
4. Why do you think we use special words to discuss something in Science?
5. List THREE words or phrases that tell you that this is a science report. Give a reason why you think so. One example has been done for you.

Word/phrase from the passage	My reason
"some things allow electricity to flow through the"	This tells me that we are conducting a science experiment.

6. Why do you think we use " " (quotation marks) when we copy words or phrases from the passage?
   _____

7. List ONE new word you learnt from each sub-heading. What does it mean? Write your own sentence using the new word.

Sub-heading	New word	Meaning	Write your own sentence using the word.
1			
2			
3			
4			
5			
6			
7			
8			
9			

8. What did you do to find the meaning of new words?
   _____

9. Draw and explain what each of the materials below were used for during this experiment.

Material	Picture	What it was used for
Crocodile clip		
Light bulb		
Battery		
Aluminium wire		
Balloon		

B: Sentence Level

Answer the questions using complete sentences.

1. Why do you think there is a date on this report?
   _____

2. Why do we need an introduction?
   _____

3. What is this science report about?
   _____

4. Why do you think knowing about conductors and insulators can save lives?
   _____

5. Look at the hypothesis:
   a. Why do you think we need a hypothesis in a science report?
      _____
   b. Did this experiment fulfill the hypothesis? How do you know this?
      _____

6. List three sentences from the discussion paragraph that give us important information about this experiment.
   a. _____
   b. _____
   c. _____

7. Answer the questions below:

Why do you think there is a warning at the end of the method?	
Do you think all science reports need to have warnings? Why?	

8. List THREE interesting facts about this science report. One example has been done for you.

The introduction informs us what the experiment was about.

Write your own beginning sentence for each these sub-headings.

Sub-heading	Sentence from the report	My own sentence
Introduction	Electricity is an important part of our lives.	
Discussion	Most metals were conductors of electricity and most non-metallic materials were insulators.	

C: Text Level

Write ONE sentence to show what each sub-heading is about. Then answer the two questions.

Sub-heading 1	
Sub-heading 2	
Sub-heading 3	
Sub-heading 4	
Sub-heading 5	
Sub-heading 6	
Sub-heading 7	
Sub-heading 8	
Sub-heading 9	
Think about how the writer has written about different things under each sub-heading. a. How does each sub-heading and the information under that connect to the title? b. How will you use this idea in your own writing?	a. b.

Functional Grammar

	Describe	What?	Extra Information
A	safe	electricity	supply is important.
		materials	
		clip wires	
		plastic bottle	
		metal	
		oil	
		experiment	

D: Writing

Conduct a simple experiment. Write your own Science Report about it. Use the sub-headings to help you plan.

Title	
Introduction - What is _____? - What do we know about it?	
Aim	
Hypothesis	
Materials	
Method	
Diagram	
Results	
Discussion	
Conclusion	

Part Four – Advanced/Consolidating Level – Science Report

Genre 1, Text 2

Teacher's Notes: What is a Science Report?

A science report presents the results of scientific research or experimentation. The purpose of a science report is to communicate scientific findings and to provide a clear and accurate summary of the methods, results, and conclusions of the study.

Science reports can take many forms, such as lab reports, research papers, scientific articles, and technical reports. They often include a description of the research question or hypothesis, the methods used to conduct the study, the results of the study, and a discussion of the significance and implications of the findings.

When writing a science report, it is important to use clear and concise language, and to organise the information in a logical and coherent manner. The report should include a description of the procedures and techniques used in the study, as well as any data, graphs, or other visual aids that help to illustrate the findings.

For English as an Additional Language/Dialect (EAL/D) students, science reports can be a valuable tool for developing research and presentation skills, as well as for communicating scientific information in a clear and accessible way. They are an effective way to build objective research and academic writing skills.

Features of a Science Report

- Includes Title and Abstract/Summary of the investigation.
- Introduction – provides background information, research question, and hypothesis.
- Aim – explains why an experiment is being conducted.
- Hypothesis – what is the predicted result?
- Materials – a list of all the materials needed.
- Method – a step by step of what was done.
- Result – may include graphs, tables, diagrams, pictures etc.
- Discussion – what was found and what else could have happened?
- Conclusion – main findings, what that means, future possibilities, etc.
- Reference – articles, textbooks, etc.
- Accurate and factual – based on experiments/research.
- Clearly and logically organised – may include heading, sub-headings, images with captions, conclusion etc.
- Objective language – more facts, less personal opinions.
- Language features – metalanguage, technical terms, etc.

Text 2 – Science Report

Lifecycle of a Bean Plant

Writing a science report about the lifecycle of a bean plant allows students to watch and record an experiment in real time. Recording and writing a lifecycle science report can help EAL/D students explore and discuss the connection between all living things. This will help set them up for future science report writing and is an example of how we can teach English using cross-curricular subject areas. Writing simple science reports at the advanced level allows students to experiment with fundamental skills for academic research and non-fiction work.

Part Four, Genre 1 – Science Report
The Lifecycle of a Bean Plant

Word Bank

pollution	dirt and dust in the air
eventually	in the end
extinct	died out
harvested	collected
germination	seed breaking for the plant to start to grow.
seedling	baby plant
conditions/environment	what is happening in and around the plant.
time-consuming	takes a lot of time

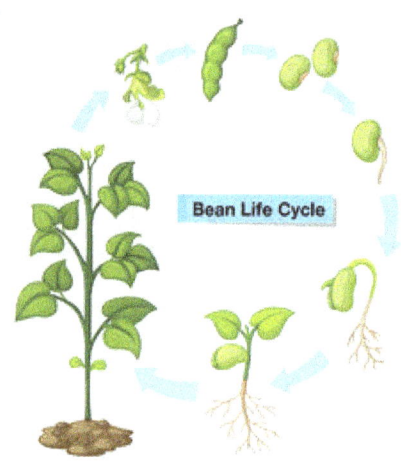
Bean Life Cycle

Model Text – Annotated for whole class discussion

Structure	Science Report	Language Features
Title Date	Title: Lifecycle of a Bean Plant Date: 1st April 2023 to 30 April 2023	Title – tells us what the experiment is about. Date – tells us when this experiment was conducted and helps us to compare with past or future similar experiments.
Introduction We are introducing the topic.	Plants are an important part of our food chain. Plants contribute food and oxygen to all living beings. They also clean our air and remove carbon dioxide and other types of pollution. Without plants, life on earth will eventually go extinct. Did you know that all plants have their own life cycles?	Gives a little background about the experiment. Present tense.
Aim	The aim of this experiment is to watch and record the different stages of the lifecycle of a bean plant.	• States the purpose of the experiment – just one or two sentences. • Present tense.
Hypothesis	There will be many stages before the bean plant gives us beans.	• Prediction of the result – one or two sentences. • Present tense.
Materials	• Bean seeds • Soil • Glass bottle	• List of all the materials used in the experiment.
Method	1. The seed was planted in a glass bottle filled with soil. 2. The bottle was placed where there was sunlight. 3. The seed was watered daily. 4. The growth of the seed was drawn and recorded in a journal. 5. The plant was allowed to grow until the beans could be harvested.	• Step by step of what was done. • Sequential from first to last step. • Past tense

Unlocking Genre

Diagram						• Shows what happened in the experiment. • Labels tell us processes took place. • The diagram can be drawn by hand as in this example.
	Life Cycle of a Bean (hand-drawn diagram showing Seed in soil → Germination with root → Seedling with leaves → Flowering Plant with stem, leaves, roots → Adult Plant with bean pods → Bean pods with seeds, cycling back to Seed)					
Results	Picture	Label	What we could see	Explanation		• Usually written in a table format. • Tells us what we saw and noted during the experiment.
	seed in soil	Seed	We could see the seed on one side of the bottle. It was covered in soil.	The seed was planted and ready to grow.		
	seed with root growing into soil	Germination	We could see that the skin of the seed was breaking and a small root was growing down into the soil.	The seed had enough water and warmth from the sun to germinate. The root was going into the soil to absorb water and nutrients to help the seed grow.		
	seedling with leaves, soil, roots	Seedling	Two leaves and a stem were coming out of the soil.	The bean seed was now a seedling. It was pushing out the stem and the leaves to help the plant get more energy from the sunlight through the process of		

Unlocking Genre   160

				photosynthesis. During this process the green chlorophyl inside the leaves use sunlight, carbon dioxide, and water to make food to help the plant to continue growing.	
		Flowering Plant	The stem was taller and stronger. There were more leaves and a flower had bloomed. We had to put the bean plants out in the garden.	The bean seed was now a flowering plant. We put the plants out in the garden so they could grow stronger and produce beans.	
		Adult Plant	The plant was strong and the flowers had changed into bean pods.	The bean seed had grown into an adult plant. The flowers of the plants had changed into bean pods.	
		Bean Pod	There were beans inside the bean pods.	These beans could be dried and used as seeds again so the lifecycle of the bean plant could continue.	
Discussion	It took time for the lifecycle of the bean plant to go from a seed to an adult plant. The bean plant needed the right conditions such as daily watering, sunlight, and a good soil for it to grow well. We could have put a seed in a dark place to compare how different				• Reflecting on what happened

	environments could affect the process. If we took care of plants that give us food, we could have a continuous supply of nourishment.	during the experiment. • Thinking about what else we could have done. • Any new or future possibilities. • Past tense.
Conclusion	The lifecycle of a bean plant was a complex and time-consuming process involving germination, seedling growth, photosynthesis, and finally seed production. Understanding this lifecycle is important for life on earth.	• Short statement. • Linked to the aim. • Past tense.

Discussion questions:

1. Where do you think this experiment took place?
2. What does the title tell us? Do you think it is important to have a title/ Why?
3. What does the date tell us? Why is this important in a science report?
4. How do the sub-headings help us?
5. What do you already know about science reports?
6. Think about a science experiment that you would like to conduct. What would you do first?
7. List three benefits of plants.

Model Text – Non-Annotated

Title: Lifecycle of a Bean Plant
Date: 1st April 2023 to 30 April 2023

Introduction
Plants are an important part of our food chain. Plants contribute food and oxygen to all living beings. They also clean our air and remove carbon dioxide and other types of pollution. Without plants, life on earth will eventually go extinct. Did you know that all plants have their own life cycles?

Aim
The aim of this experiment is to watch and record the different stages of the lifecycle of a bean plant.

Hypothesis
There will be many stages before the bean plant gives us beans.

Materials
- Bean seeds
- Soil
- Glass bottle

Method
1. The seed was planted in a glass bottle filled with soil.
2. The bottle was placed where there was sunlight.
3. The seed was watered daily.
4. The growth of the seed was drawn and recorded in a journal.
5. The plant was allowed to grow until the beans could be harvested.

Diagram

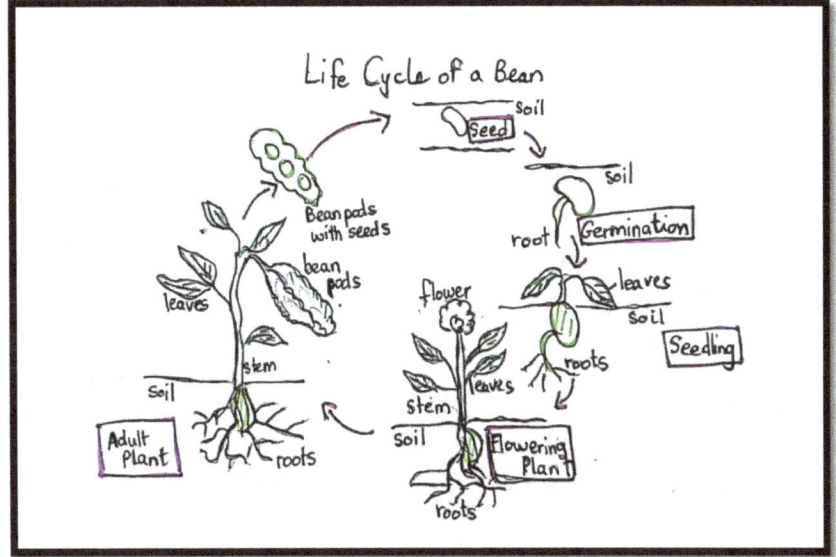

Results

Picture	Label	What we could see	Explanation
	Seed	We could see the seed on one side of the bottle. It was covered in soil.	The seed was planted and ready to grow.
	Germination	We could see that the skin of the seed was breaking and a small root was growing down into the soil.	The seed had enough water and warmth from the sun to germinate. The root was going into the soil to absorb water and nutrients to help the seed grow.
	Seedling	Two leaves and a stem were coming out of the soil.	The bean seed was now a seedling. It was pushing out the stem and the leaves to help the plant get more energy from the sunlight through the process of photosynthesis. During this process the green chlorophyl inside the leaves use sunlight, carbon dioxide, and water to make food to help the plant to continue growing.
	Flowering Plant	The stem was taller and stronger. There were more leaves and a flower had bloomed. We had to put the bean plants out in the garden.	The bean seed was now a flowering plant. We put the plants out in the garden so they could grow stronger produce beans.

Unlocking Genre   163

	Adult Plant	The plant was strong and the flowers had changed into bean pods.	The bean seed had grown into an adult plant. The flowers of the plants had changed into bean pods.
	Bean Pod	There were beans inside the bean pods.	These beans could be dried and used as seeds again so the lifecycle of the bean plant could continue.

Discussion

It took time for the lifecycle of the bean plant to go from a seed to an adult plant. The bean plant needed the right conditions such as daily watering, sunlight, and a good soil for it to grow well. We could have put a seed in a dark place to compare how different environments could affect the process. If we took care of plants that give us food, we could have a continuous supply of nourishment.

Conclusion

The lifecycle of a bean plant was a complex and time-consuming process involving germination, seedling growth, photosynthesis, and finally seed production. Understanding this lifecycle is important for life on earth.

Reading and Viewing Activities

A: Word Level

1. List all the verbs you can see.

2. The verbs are written in the _____ tense because _____.
3. What does the word 'lifecycle' mean?
4. What other lifecycles can you think of?
5. Why do you think we use special words to discuss something in Science?
6. List THREE words or phrases that tell you that this is a science report. Give a reason why you think so. One example has been done for you.

Word/phrase from the passage	My reason
"the aim of this experiment is…"	This tells me that we are conducting a science experiment.

7. List ONE new word you learnt from each sub-heading. What does it mean? Write your own sentence using the new word.

Sub-heading	New word	Meaning	Write your own sentence using the word.
1			
2			
3			
4			
5			
6			
7			
8			
9			

8. What did you do to find the meaning of new words?
   _____

9. Draw and explain what each of the materials below were used for during this experiment.

Material	Picture	What it was used for
Bean seeds		
Soil		
Glass bottle		

B: Sentence Level

Answer the questions using complete sentences.

1. Why do you think there is a date on this report?
   _____

2. Why do we need an introduction?
   _____

3. What is this science report about?
   _____

4. Why do you think knowing about plant lifecycles can save lives?
   _____

5. Look at the hypothesis:
   a. Why do you think we need a hypothesis in a science report?
      _____
   b. Did this experiment fulfill the hypothesis? How do you know this?
      _____

6. List three events from the result table that give us important information about this experiment.
   a. _____
   b. _____
   c. _____

7. Answer the questions below:

Do you think all plant life cycles would produce food?	
Explain your answer.	

8. List THREE interesting facts about this science report. One example has been done for you.

Plants make their own food through the process of photosynthesis.

Write your own beginning sentence for each these sub-headings.

Sub-heading	Sentence from the report	My own sentence
Introduction	Plants are an important part of our food chain.	
Discussion	It took time for the lifecycle of the bean plant to go from a seed to an adult plant.	

C: Text Level

Write ONE sentence to show what each sub-heading is about. Then answer the two questions.

Sub-heading 1	
Sub-heading 2	
Sub-heading 3	
Sub-heading 4	
Sub-heading 5	
Sub-heading 6	
Sub-heading 7	
Sub-heading 8	
Sub-heading 9	
Think about how the writer has written about different things under each sub-heading. a. How does each sub-heading and the information under that connect to the title? b. How will you use this idea in your own writing?	a. b.

Functional Grammar

	Describe	What?	Extra Information
Our	important	food chain	keeps us alive.
		pollution	
		experiment	
		bean plant	
		soil	
		roots	
		stem	

D: Writing

Conduct a simple experiment. Write your own Science Report about it. Use the sub-headings to help you plan.

Title	
Introduction - What is _____ ? - What do we know about it?	
Aim	
Hypothesis	
Materials	
Method	
Diagram	
Results	
Discussion	
Conclusion	

Part Four – Advanced/Consolidating Level – Text Analysis

Genre 2, Text 1

Teacher's Notes: What is a Text Analysis?

Text analysis is the process of examining a written, spoken, or film text to gain a deeper understanding of its content, structure, and meaning. It involves analysing the language, syntax, grammar, and other literary elements to identify patterns, themes, and other technical features that help to reveal the author's message or intent.

When analysing a text, it is important to consider the context in which it was produced, including the author's background, the intended audience, and the social and cultural factors that may have influenced its creation. Analysing films include identifying the use of filmic devices, themes, and interpreting the meaning behind direct and inferential messages.

For English as an Additional Language/Dialect (EAL/D) students, text analysis is an important skill that can help them develop critical thinking and analytical skills, as well as improve their ability to communicate effectively. It is commonly used in fields such as literature, media studies, linguistics, and communication studies, as well as in business, politics, and other areas where effective communication is important.

Features of a Text Analysis – Film

- Introduction – provides background information about the film (title, year produced, language, director), its genre, overall message, and its context.
- Summary – a brief summary of the text highlighting:
    - setting
    - key themes
    - ideas
    - messages.
- Analysis of:
    - Content – the film's use of themes, symbols, motifs, etc.
    - Filmic Techniques – Camera angles, sounds, theme, subject matter etc.
    - Plot and structure – linear or nonlinear, suspense, important sequences, etc.
    - Conflict – internal and external.
    - Characterisation – through dialogue, appearance, interactions, personality qualities and development, stereotypes, etc.
    - Narration – is there a narrator, whose point of view
    - Symbolism, imagery, inferences, etc.
- Evidence to support the analysis – specific examples, quotes, etc.
- Conclusion – main findings, what that means, etc.
- Accurate – based on the film being analysed.
- Clearly and logically organised – may include heading, sub-headings, conclusion etc.
- Objective and subjective language – facts and personal opinions.
- Language features – metalanguage, technical terms, etc.

Text 1 – Text Analysis
Film – Moana

Writing a text analysis about a film allows students to critically examine and evaluate a text by deconstructing its content, structure, and language features. Analysing a film can help EAL/D students explore and discuss literary devices that exist in the English language. This will create awareness of the nuances of the language and encourage them to take risks in their daily writing tasks. Writing simple text analysis at the advanced level allows students to go deeper into experimenting with the fundamental skills for creative writing.

Part Four, Genre 2 – Text Analysis
Moana
Directed by Ron Clements and John Musker
Produced by Walt Disney Animation Studios

Word Bank

animated film	A movie made from drawings, computer pictures or photos.
fantasy	Something we create from our imagination.
Polynesia	A group of islands in the Pacific Ocean
curse	Words that cause harm
demigod	A less important god
culture	A way of life
attempted	Tried
depiction	Showing as an example.
traditional	Old way of doing something.
authentic	Real
portrayal	Showing something.
emphasises	Making sure we pay attention to it.
interconnectedness	Everything is connected to each other.
echoing	Repeating
protagonist	Main character
determined	Wanting to do something and not changing our mind.
independent	Thinking and making decisions for ourselves.
resourceful	Can find answers.
selfish	Only caring about yourself.
unreliable	Cannot be trusted.
immortal	Cannot die.
mythical	Stories and characters made up from our imagination.
vibrant	Bright
visually stunning	Very beautiful to look at.
perseverance	Not giving up.
resonates	Brings up images, memories, emotions...

Unlocking Genre 169

Model Text – Annotated for whole class discussion

Structure	Text Analysis	Language Features
Title **Year** **Producer** **Directors** **Co-Directors**	Moana 2016 Walt Disney Animations Studio Ron Clement and John Musker Don Hall and Chris Williams	**Title** – tells us what the film is called. **Year** – the year the film was released. **Producer** – Films have producers who give money for the film to be made. **Directors/Co-directors** – we need to name the people who directed the film.
Introduction We are introducing the film.	*Moana* is a 2016 Disney animated fantasy film that tells the story of a young Polynesian girl who sets out on a brave journey to restore the heart of Te Fiti, a mountain goddess, in order to save her people from a devastating curse. During this journey, Moana looks for the demigod Maui, who is the thief of Te Fiti's heart. She finds Maui and forces him to guide her on her journey as they sail together across the South Pacific ocean. One of the strengths of *Moana* is its representation of Polynesian and Tongan culture, which has not been really attempted by Disney before. From the music and language to the depiction of traditional practices such as wayfinding and tattooing, the film offers a respectful and authentic portrayal of this often overlooked part of the world. Additionally, the film emphasises the importance of community and the interconnectedness of all living things, echoing the values of many Pacific Island cultures.	We type the name of the film in *italics*. Present tense. The genre of the film. Metalanguage for film analysis.
Characters Discussing some of the main characters.	The character Moana, the film's protagonist, is a determined, independent, and resourceful young woman who defies the expectations of her community in order to follow her own values. Moana's grandmother supports and encourages her to fulfil her destiny and discover who she really is. Maui, the immortal demigod who accompanies Moana on her journey, is initially selfish and unreliable but learns the value of humility and sacrifice over the course of the story.	Present tense. The characters we are focusing on. The characteristics of the main characters. Metalanguage for film analysis.
Music and Animation Some filmic techniques that have been used in this film.	Traditional Polynesian music is played right at the beginning of the film. This immediately connects the audience to the cultural setting of the movie. All the songs in *Moana* are a mix of traditional Polynesian music, sung in both English and the Polynesian language. This further helps the audience to understand the rich musical culture of the Polynesian people. The animation in *Moana* presents a mythical, vibrant, and visually stunning adventure of talking creatures, gods and	Present tense. Metalanguage for film analysis. What do the music and animation do to connect to the audience.

Unlocking Genre

	goddesses, and a living ocean that showcases the rich cultural heritage of the Pacific Islands. It is a great example of how animation can be used to explore complex themes and cultural beliefs around the world.	
Themes We are exploring the message that the writers and directors want to convey to the audience.	*Moana* represents the courage, perseverance, and adventurous spirit of the Polynesian and Tongan people of the past. It shows us that remembering our roots and our ancestors can help us discover who we truly are, like how Moana did when she was fighting Te Ka, the demon of fire. Moana, the main character does not allow her father to determine how she should live her life. This rebellion leads Moana on an adventure that eventually saves her island from dying. This storyline shows us that sometimes we may need to be brave enough to fight against existing belief systems in order to find solutions to our problems. Another theme in Moana is how natural disasters can be caused by greed and selfishness. In Moana, this is depicted through fantasy and myths. When the demigod Maui, steals the heart of Te Fiti, the island begins to die. This signifies that when we are greedy and selfish enough to 'steal' important natural resources, our earth will begin to die.	Present tense Main themes Evidence from the film.
Conclusion We bring it all together and repeat some of our analysis in the conclusion.	*Moana* is a well written movie plot with cultural characters that truly represent its message of empowerment and connection to ancestors. In my opinion, it definitely resonates with audiences of all ages.	Present tense We summarise our ideas. Personal opinion. Filmic language.

Discussion questions:

1. Why do you think this film analysis is mostly written in the present tense?
2. What does the title tell us? Do you think it is important to have a title/ Why?
3. How do the sub-headings help us?
4. What do you already know about films and text analysis?
5. Think about a film from your home country. Share the main message of the film with your friends?
6. Do you enjoy watching movies in your home language? Why?

Model Text – Non-Annotated

Film Analysis
Title of film: Moana
Year: 2016
Producer: Walt Disney Animations Studio
Directors: Ron Clement and John Musker
Co-directors: Don Hall and Chris Williams

Introduction

Moana is a 2016 Disney animated fantasy film that tells the story of a young Polynesian girl who sets out on a brave journey to restore the heart of Te Fiti, a mountain goddess, in order to save her people from a devastating curse. During this journey, Moana looks for the demigod Maui, who is the thief of Te Fiti's heart. She finds Maui and forces him to guide her on her journey as they sail together across the South Pacific ocean.

One of the strengths of *Moana* is its representation of Polynesian and Tongan culture, which has not been really attempted by Disney before. From the music and language to the depiction of traditional practices such as wayfinding and tattooing, the film offers a respectful and authentic portrayal of this often overlooked part of the world. Additionally, the film emphasises the importance of community and the interconnectedness of all living things, echoing the values of many Pacific Island cultures.

Characters

The character Moana, the film's protagonist, is a determined, independent, and resourceful young woman who defies the expectations of her community in order to follow her own values. Moana's grandmother supports and encourages her to fulfil her destiny and discover who she really is.

Maui, the immortal demigod who accompanies Moana on her journey, is initially selfish and unreliable but learns the value of humility and sacrifice over the course of the story.

Music and Animation

Traditional Polynesian music is played right at the beginning of the film. This immediately connects the audience to the cultural setting of the movie. All the songs in *Moana* are a mix of traditional Polynesian music, sung in both English and the Polynesian language. This further helps the audience to understand the rich musical culture of the Polynesian people.

The animation in *Moana* presents a mythical, vibrant, and visually stunning adventure of talking creatures, gods and goddesses, and a living ocean that showcases the rich cultural heritage of the Pacific Islands. It is a great example of how animation can be used to explore complex themes and cultural beliefs around the world.

Themes

Moana represents the courage, perseverance, and adventurous spirit of the Polynesian and Tongan people of the past. It shows us that remembering our roots and our ancestors can help us discover who we truly are, like how Moana did when she was fighting Te Ka, the demon of fire.

Moana, the main character does not allow her father to determine how she should live her life. This rebellion leads Moana on an adventure that eventually saves her island from dying. This storyline shows us that sometimes we may need to be brave enough to fight against existing belief systems in order to find solutions to our problems.

Another theme in Moana is how natural disasters can be caused by greed and selfishness. In *Moana*, this is depicted through fantasy and myths. When the demigod Maui, steals the heart of Te Fiti, the island begins to die. This signifies that when we are greedy and selfish enough to 'steal' important natural resources, our earth will begin to die.

Conclusion

Moana is a well written movie plot with cultural characters that truly represent its message of empowerment and connection to ancestors. In my opinion, it definitely resonates with audiences of all ages.

Reading and Viewing Activities

A: Word Level

1. List all the verbs you can see.

2. The verbs are written in the _____ tenses because _____.
3. What do the words 'themes' and 'characters' mean?
4. Why do you think we use special words to analyse a film?
5. List THREE words or phrases that tell you that this is a text analysis. Give a reason why you think so. One example has been done for you.

Word/phrase from the passage	My reason
"*Moana* is a ....."	This tells me that we are analysing a film.

6. Why do you think we use " " (quotation marks) when we copy words or phrases from the film?
   _____

7. List ONE new word you learnt from each sub-heading. What does it mean? Write your own sentence using the new word.

Sub-heading	New word	Meaning	Write your own sentence using the word.
Introduction			
Characters			
Music and Animation			
Themes			
Conclusion			

8. What did you do to find the meaning of new words?
   _____

9. Give an example from the film analysis for each filmic technique below. Explain how it helps the audience.

Filmic Technique	Example	How does it help the audience?
animation		
music		

Unlocking Genre 173

B: Sentence Level

Answer the questions using complete sentences.

1. Why do you think we need to acknowledge the producer and the directors of the film?
   _____

2. Why do we need an introduction?
   _____

3. What is this text analysis about?
   _____

4. Why do you think we analyse different aspects of the film?
   _____

5. Look at the themes:
   a. Why do you think we need to analyse themes in a film analysis?
      _____
   b. How do the themes help us analyse this film? How do you know this?
      _____

6. List three sentences from the introduction section that give us important information about this film.
   a. _____
   b. _____
   c. _____

7. Answer the questions below:

What do we do in the conclusion of a text analysis?	
Does the analysis help the reader understand the film better? Why?	

8. List THREE interesting ideas about this text analysis. One example has been done for you.

The introduction informs us what the film is about.

Write your own beginning sentence for each these sub-headings.

Sub-heading	Sentence from the analysis	My own sentence
Introduction	*Moana* is a 2016 Disney animated fantasy film that tells the story of a young Polynesian girl who sets out on a brave journey to restore the heart of Te Fiti, a mountain goddess, in order to save her people from a devastating curse."	
Conclusion	*Moana* is a well written movie plot with cultural characters that truly represent its message of empowerment and connection to ancestors.	

C: Text Level
Write ONE sentence to explain what each sub-heading is about. Then answer the two questions.

Introduction	
Characters	
Music and Animation	
Themes	
Conclusion	
Think about how the writer has written about different things under each sub-heading. a. How does each sub-heading and the information under that connect to a text analysis? b. How will you use this idea in your own writing?	a. b.

Functional Grammar

	Describe	What?	Extra Information
An	interesting	film	about teachers.
		goddess	
		journey	
		woman	
		music	
		character	
		earth	

D: Writing
Choose a whole class animation film (Teacher's choice). Write your own Text Analysis about it. Use the sub-headings to help you plan.

Title of film: Year: Producer: Directors:	
Introduction	
Characters	
Music and Animation	
Themes	
Conclusion	

Unlocking Genre 175

Part Four – Advanced/Consolidating Level – Text Analysis

Genre 2, Text 2

Teacher's Notes: What is a Text Analysis?

Text analysis is the process of examining a written, spoken, or film text to gain a deeper understanding of its content, structure, and meaning. It involves analysing the language, syntax, grammar, and other literary elements to identify patterns, themes, and other technical features that help to reveal the author's message or intent.

When analysing a text, it is important to consider the context in which it was produced, including the author's background, the intended audience, and the social and cultural factors that may have influenced its creation. Common techniques used in text analysis include identifying the use of literary devices, analysing the structure of the text, and interpreting the meaning of specific words and phrases.

For English as an Additional Language/Dialect (EAL/D) students, text analysis is an important skill that can help them develop critical thinking and analytical skills, as well as improve their ability to communicate effectively. It is commonly used in fields such as literature, media studies, linguistics, and communication studies, as well as in business, politics, and other areas where effective communication is important.

Features of a Text Analysis – Poetry

- Introduction – provides background information about the author, the text, and its context.
- Summary – a brief summary of the text highlighting key themes, ideas, and messages.
- Analysis of:
    - Content – the author's use of themes, symbols, motifs, etc.
    - Structure – organisation, theme, subject matter etc.
    - Language – author's tone, style, imagery, etc.
- Evidence to support the analysis – specific examples, quotes, etc.
- Conclusion – main findings, what that means, etc.
- Accurate – based on the poem being analysed.
- Clearly and logically organised – may include heading, sub-headings, conclusion etc.
- Objective and subjective language – facts and personal opinions.
- Language features – metalanguage, technical terms, etc.

Text 2 – Text Analysis

Poem – The Road Not Taken by Robert Frost

Writing a text analysis about a poem allows students to critically examine and evaluate a text by deconstructing its content, structure, and language features. Analysing a poem can help EAL/D students explore and discuss literary devices that exist in the English language. This will create awareness of the nuances of the language and encourage them to take risks in their daily writing tasks. Writing simple text analysis at the advanced level allows students to go deeper into experimenting with the fundamental skills for creative writing.

Part Four, Genre 2 – Text Analysis
The Road Not Taken
By Robert Lee Frost

Word Bank

interpreted	Can be explained or thought of in different ways
stanzas	We use the word stanza when talking about a "paragraph" in a poem.
rhyme	When the ending of words sound similar.
theme	What subject matter or issue the poet is writing about.
poetic device	Tools and ideas used by a poet to help the reader to have a deeper understanding of a poem.
symbolism	Using normal words to mean something else.
imagery	Using words to help the reader imagine a place, situation, or thought in a poem.
metaphor	Using words and ideas to create a "story", or thoughts for the reader.
consequences	Result of an action.

Unlocking Genre

Model Text – Annotated for whole class discussion

The Road Not Taken
By Robert Lee Frost

Two roads diverged in a yellow wood,
And sorry I could not travel both
And be one traveler, long I stood
And looked down one as far as I could
To where it bent in the undergrowth;

Then took the other, as just as fair
And having perhaps the better claim,
Because it was grassy and wanted wear;
Though as for that, the passing there
Had worn them really about the same,

And both that morning equally lay
In leaves no step had trodden black
Oh, I kept the first for another day!
Yet knowing how way leads on to way,
I doubted if I should ever come back.

I shall be telling this with a sigh
Somewhere ages and ages hence:
Two roads diverged in a wood, and I,
I took the one less traveled by,
And that has made all the difference.

Structure	Text Analysis	Language Features
Title **Author**	**The Road Not Taken** **By Robert Lee Frost**	Title – tells us what the poem is called. The title usually gives the reader an idea of what the poem may be about. Author – tells us who wrote the poem.
Introduction We are introducing the poem.	"The Road Not Taken" was written by Robert Frost in 1915. It is a very famous poem that has been interpreted differently by individuals over the years. The poet wrote about making a choice of a less travelled road when he came across two roads. We can look at "The Road Not Taken" from many different sides. It could be about making difficult choices and facing the consequences of our actions. It also makes the reader think what could have happened to the poet if he had taken the other road. The poem has four stanzas with five lines each. They are written in the 'ABAAB' rhyme. This means the first, third, and fourth line end with the same sounds, and the second and last line end with the same sounds.	We use quotation marks when typing or handwriting titles of poems. Past participle/passive voice and past tense. Present tense. A little information about – what the poem is about? Metalanguage for poetry analysis.

Unlocking Genre   178

Summary Additional information about each stanza. We are summarising and analysing what the poet may be thinking. We can do this by exploring each stanza on its own.	In the first stanza, Frost seems to be walking along a path when he comes to a fork in the road where the path splits into two different roads. It is most likely during autumn as he says that he is in a "yellow wood" which means the leaves are turning yellow. He is alone as "one traveler" so he could not walk on both paths. He stands and looks at both roads for a long time. However, he is unable to see far as the "undergrowth" is blocking his view. In the second stanza, the poet decides that both paths are equally good and chooses one that seems less used and "grassy", to continue his walk. However, he also thinks that they may both have been equally used by others who had walked there before him. In stanza three, the poet talks about how the colour of the leaves on both paths revealed that no one had walked over them yet. He decides on taking the second one and keep "the first for another day!" However, he understands that one path will lead to another and doubts that he would "ever come back" to the first road. In the final stanza, the poet imagines that somewhere in the distant future, he would be telling the story of how he chose one road over the other. He will remember how this choice has "made all the difference" in his life.	Present tense Using the poet's last name when talking about his poem. A short summary is provided for each stanza. Inferencing with evidence from the poem. What the poet does and thinks about – we add quotes from the poem to support our analysis. Although the poem is written in the first person (I), we use the third person (he, him) in our analysis.
Themes We are exploring the message that the poet wants to convey to his readers.	The themes of this poem are centred around personal choices and their consequences. The poet feels "sorry" that he could not take both roads and has to make a difficult decision. Frost is thinking how choosing one road over the other could "make all the difference" in his life many years in the future. This tells us that all our choices have consequences and may affect the rest of our lives.	Present tense Main themes Evidence for the first theme - personal choices Evidence for the second theme (with a quote from the poem) – consequences of our personal choices.

Poetic Devices Poets often use a variety of techniques like the ones below to allow the reader to experience their poems on a deeper level. **Symbolism** We are analysing how the poet using his words to mean something important. **Imagery** – allows the reader to use their senses and imagine the scenery. **Metaphor** – allows the reader to dig deeper into what the poet may mean.	The main symbol in this poem is the "road". The fork in the path leading to two different roads symbolises the choices we may need to make in our daily lives, including our food, clothes, and even our relationships. The other symbol is the "undergrowth" that does not allow the poet to see the rest of the road from where he is standing. This could symbolise how it is difficult to predict the future results of our current decisions. **Imagery** – Frost uses the colour yellow to describe the woods where he is walking. This allows the reader to imagine that it is autumn and the leaves are turning yellow. **Metaphor** - Taking the road "less travelled" is a metaphor showing that we need to be brave enough to make decisions based on our own thoughts and not just follow what everyone else is doing. Its setting in the season of autumn is also a metaphor of change because tress shed their leaves in order to get ready for winter. So, choosing one road over the other, could also mean that the poet is ready to make a change in his life.	Present tense Highlighting the two or three symbols – we use words from the poem to do this. Adding details and our own thoughts to the symbols we are analysing. Present tense Using colour to allow the reader to imagine the forest turning yellow in autumn. Discussing the first metaphor – linking the idea of a road that has not been used by many people to doing things for ourselves, not because everyone else is doing it. Discussing the second metaphor - linking the setting of autumn to change and analysing that this could mean that the poet wants to choose a new path for his life.
Conclusion We bring it all together and repeat some of our analysis in the conclusion.	"The Road Not Taken" is a poem that makes us think about the choices we make in life. Even if a decision seems as easy as picking one path over another, the consequences of our choices could "make all the difference" in the future. It tells us to be brave when we cannot see the future and taking the road "less traveled" could be a good thing for us.	Present tense We summarise our ideas. We use quotes from the poem to support our conclusion.

Discussion questions:

1. Discuss all the different tenses used in the analysis? How do you feel about this?
2. What does the title tell us? Do you think it is important to have a title/ Why?
3. How do the sub-headings help us?
4. What do you already know about poems and text analysis?
5. Think about a song or poem from your home country. Share the main message of the song or poem with your friends?
6. Do you enjoy reading poems in your home language? Why?

Model Text – Non-Annotated

Text analysis
The Road Not Taken
By Robert Lee Frost

Two roads diverged in a yellow wood,
And sorry I could not travel both
And be one traveler, long I stood
And looked down one as far as I could
To where it bent in the undergrowth;

Then took the other, as just as fair
And having perhaps the better claim,
Because it was grassy and wanted wear;
Though as for that, the passing there
Had worn them really about the same,

And both that morning equally lay
In leaves no step had trodden black
Oh, I kept the first for another day!
Yet knowing how way leads on to way,
I doubted if I should ever come back.

I shall be telling this with a sigh
Somewhere ages and ages hence:
Two roads diverged in a wood, and I,
I took the one less traveled by,
And that has made all the difference.

Introduction

"The Road Not Taken" was written by Robert Frost in 1915. It is a very famous poem that has been interpreted differently by individuals over the years. The poet writes about making a choice of a less travelled road when he came across two roads. We can look at "The Road Not Taken" from many different sides. It could be about making difficult choices and facing the consequences of our actions. It also makes the reader think what could have happened to the poet if he had taken the other road.

The poem has four stanzas with five lines each. They are written in the 'ABAAB' rhyme. This means the first, third, and fourth line end with the same sounds, and the second and last line end with the same sounds.

Summary

In the first stanza, Frost seems to be walking along a path when he comes to a fork in the road where the path splits into two different roads. It is most likely during autumn as he says that he is in a "yellow wood" which means the leaves are turning yellow. He is alone as "one traveler" so he could not walk on both paths. He stands and looks at both roads for a long time. However, he is unable to see far as the "undergrowth" is blocking his view.

In the second stanza, the poet decides that both paths are equally good and chooses one that seems less used and "grassy", to continue his walk. However, he also thinks that they may both have been equally used by others who had walked there before him.

In stanza three, the poet talks about how the colour of the leaves on both paths revealed that no one had walked over them yet. He decides on taking the second one and keep "the first for another day!" However, he understands that one path will lead to another and doubts that he would "ever come back" to the first road.

In the final stanza, the poet imagines that somewhere in the distant future, he would be telling the story of how he chose one road over the other. He will remember how this choice has "made all the difference" in his life.

Themes

The themes of this poem are centred around personal choices and their consequences. The poet feels "sorry" that he could not take both roads and has to make a difficult decision. Frost is thinking how choosing one road over the other could "make all the difference" in his life many years in the future. This tells us that all our choices have consequences and may affect the rest of our lives.

Poetic Devices

Symbolism

The main symbol in this poem is the road. The fork in the path leading to two different roads symbolises the choices we may need to make in our daily lives, including our food, clothes, and even our relationships.

The other symbol is the "undergrowth" that does not allow the poet to see the rest of the road from where he is standing. This could symbolise how it is difficult to predict the future results of our current decisions.

Imagery – Frost uses the colour yellow to describe the woods where he is walking. This allows the reader to imagine that it is autumn and the leaves are turning yellow.

Metaphor – Taking the road "less travelled" is a metaphor showing that we need to be brave enough to make decisions based on our own thoughts and not just follow what everyone else is doing. Its setting in the season of autumn is also a metaphor of change because tress shed their leaves in order to get ready for winter. So, choosing one road over the other, could also mean that the poet is ready to make a change in his life.

Conclusion

"The Road Not Taken" is a poem that makes us think about the choices we make in life. Even if a decision seems as easy as picking one path over another, the consequences of our choices could "make all the difference" in the future. It tells us to be brave when we cannot see the future and taking the road "less traveled" could be a good thing for us.

Reading and Viewing Activities

A: Word Level

1. List all the verbs you can see.

   [   ]

2. The verbs are written in different tenses because _____.
3. What do the words 'themes' and 'imagery' mean?
4. Why do you think we use special words to analyse a poem?
5. List THREE words or phrases that tell you that this is a text analysis. Give a reason why you think so. One example has been done for you.

Word/phrase from the passage	My reason
"The poet writes about"	This tells me that we are analysing what the poet has written.

6. Why do you think we use " " (quotation marks) when we copy words or phrases from the poem?

   _____

7. List ONE new word you learnt from each sub-heading. What does it mean? Write your own sentence using the new word.

Sub-heading	New word	Meaning	Write your own sentence using the word.
Introduction			
Summary			
Themes			
Symbolism			
Imagery			
Metaphor			
Conclusion			

8. What did you do to find the meaning of new words?

   _____

9. Give an example from the poem for each poetic device below. Explain how it helps the reader.

Poetic Device	Example	How does it help the reader?
Symbolism		
Imagery		
Metaphor		

B: Sentence Level

Answer the questions using complete sentences.

1. Why do you think we acknowledge the author's name?
   _____

2. Why do we need an introduction?
   _____

3. What is this text analysis about?
   _____

4. Why do you think we analyse so many different aspects of the poem?
   _____

5. Look at the summary:
   a. Why do you think we need a summary in a text analysis?
      _____
   b. How does the summary help us analyse this poem? How do you know this?
      _____

6. List three sentences from the poetic devices section that give us important information about this poem.
   a. _____
   b. _____
   c. _____

7. Answer the questions below:

What do we do in the conclusion of a text analysis?	
Does the analysis help the reader understand the poem better? Why?	

8. List THREE interesting ideas about this text analysis. One example has been done for you.

The introduction informs us what the poem is about.

Write your own beginning sentence for each these sub-headings.

Sub-heading	Sentence from the analysis	My own sentence
Introduction	"The Road Not Taken" was written by Robert Frost in 1915.	
Conclusion	"The Road Not Taken" is a poem that makes us think about the choices we make in life.	

C: Text Level

Write ONE sentence to show what each sub-heading is about. Then answer the two questions.

Introduction	
Summary	
Themes	
Poetic Devices	
Conclusion	
Think about how the writer has written about different things under each sub-heading. a. How does each sub-heading and the information under that connect to a text analysis? b. How will you use this idea in your own writing?	a. b.

Functional Grammar

	Describe	What?	Extra Information
A	famous	poem	written by Robert Frost
		road	
		choices	
		stanza	
		leaves	
		paths	
		decision	

D: Writing

Choose a whole class poem (Teacher's choice). Write your own Text Analysis about it. Use the sub-headings to help you plan.

Title Author	
Introduction	
Summary	
Themes (2 or 3)	
Poetic Devices (2 or 3)	
Conclusion	

Part Four – Advanced/Consolidating Level – Language Analysis
Genre 3, Text 1
Teacher's Notes: What is a Language Analysis?

Language analysis is the study of how language is used to convey meaning, and influence or persuade readers. It involves analysing written or spoken language to identify syntax and semantics, literary techniques, and linguistic strategies that a writer or speaker uses to communicate a particular message or idea.

Language analysis can take many forms, such as literary analysis, discourse analysis, and rhetorical analysis. It can involve analysing the use of language in a single text or across a range of texts or genres. It is commonly used in fields such as literature, media studies, linguistics, and communication studies, as well as in business, politics, and other areas where effective communication is important.

When analysing language, it is important to consider the context in which it is used, including the audience, the purpose of the text, and the cultural and social factors that may influence its interpretation. Common techniques used in language analysis include identifying the use of figurative language, rhetorical devices, and persuasive appeals such as logos (logic), ethos (credibility), and pathos (emotional connection).

For English as an Additional Language/Dialect (EAL/D) students, language analysis is an important skill that can help them develop critical thinking and analytical skills, as well as improve their ability to deconstruct the nuances of the English language more effectively. They may come across the opportunity to do this through their everyday connection with social media, news, advertisements, global issues, current trends, etc.

Features of a Language Analysis – Blog on Climate Change

- Introduction – provides background information about the blog (title, author, language), its genre, overall message, and its context.
- Summary – a brief summary of the text highlighting:
    - form
    - context
    - date
    - contention
    - audience
    - tone
    - author etc.
- Analysis of how the examples below are used to persuade the audience:
    - Content – the author's use of themes, symbols, motifs, etc.
    - Theme – author's message
    - Literary Techniques/Devices – dialogue, figurative language, imagery, etc.
- Author's Voice – sentence structure, grammar, humour, etc.
- Conflict – real, perceived, projected, etc.
- Data – author's use of graphs, numbers, etc.
- Evidence to support the analysis – specific examples, quotes, etc.
- Conclusion – main findings, what that means, personal opinion, etc.
- Accurate – based on the language being analysed.
- Clearly and logically organised – may include heading, sub-headings, conclusion etc.
- Objective and subjective language – facts and personal opinions.
- Language features – metalanguage, technical terms, etc.

Text 1 – Language Analysis
Blog – Climate Change

Writing a language analysis about a blog allows students to critically examine and evaluate a text by deconstructing its content, structure, and language features. Analysing a blog can help EAL/D students explore and discuss literary devices that exist in the English language. This will create awareness of the nuances of the language and encourage them to take risks in their daily writing tasks. Writing simple language analysis at the advanced level allows students to go deeper into experimenting with the fundamental skills for analytical writing.

Part Four, Genre 3 – Language Analysis
Blog – Climate Change

Word Bank

climate change	the change in our weather conditions
global warming	the rise in temperatures around the world
extreme	very serious
currently	at the moment
anxious	worried
contention	argument
consequences	result of our actions
irreversible	we cannot repair the damage
persuade	strongly encourage
influence	something that helps us change our minds
statistics	numbers and percentages
gigatonnes	1 gigatonne is equal to 1 billion tonnes
marginalised	not included
vulnerable	not being taken care of and may be in danger
inclusive	included in the blog
restoration	repair
ethical	moral – doing the right thing

Model Text – Annotated for whole class discussion

December 28, 2023
By Boney Nathan

Let's Cool Down and Fight for Change!

Global warming and climate change is one of the most pressing issues facing our planet today. As global temperatures continue to rise, we are seeing an increase in extreme weather events, melting ice caps, and rising sea levels. We recently saw extreme wild weather bringing large hailstones and torrential rains on the states of Victoria, New South Wales, and Queensland on Christmas and Boxing Day, leaving many without electricity and life-threatening property damage. Various other natural disasters around the world were constantly in the news headlines in 2023. These included the massive twin earthquakes in Turkey on 6 February that killed more than fifty thousand people, devastating storms that caused flooding in many parts of the world, volcanic eruptions, bushfires, and many more. Scientists think that these types of extreme weather conditions with become more serious and dangerous as our earth continues to get warmer. It is clear that action must be taken to reduce our impact on the environment and address this urgent issue.

Over 97% of scientists agree that one of the primary causes of climate change is the emission of greenhouse gases, such as carbon dioxide, methane, and nitrous oxide, from human activities like burning fossil fuels, deforestation, and agriculture. Scientists also agree that the rate of carbon emissions is the highest it has been in 66 million years. These gases trap heat in the atmosphere, leading to the greenhouse effect and resulting in the warming of the planet. According to the United Nations Environment Programme (UNEP), total greenhouse emissions in 2019 reached an extreme high of 59.1 gigatonnes of carbon dioxide. It made 2019 the second hottest year on record.

It is also important to recognise that climate change disproportionately affects marginalised communities, such as low-income and Indigenous populations, who often bear the brunt of extreme weather events and environmental degradation. According to the United Nations, 30% of the world's population is exposed to deadly heat waves more than 20 days per year. Addressing climate change must be done in a just and equitable manner, with consideration given to those who are most vulnerable.

To combat climate change, we must take action to reduce our greenhouse gas emissions. According to UNEP, we need to explore ways to continuously reduce greenhouse gas emissions by 7.6% every year up to the year 2030. This can be achieved through a combination of individual and collective efforts, including the adoption of renewable energy sources like solar and wind power, energy-efficient buildings, and sustainable transportation. Governments can also play a significant role in reducing emissions through policies to restore natural spaces both on land and in water, investments in clean energy infrastructure, and setting targets and timelines to lower their dependency on energy produced by carbon fuel.

The impact of climate change is already being felt around the world, but it is not too late to take action. By reducing our greenhouse gas emissions and transitioning to a more sustainable way of life, we can help reduce the worst effects of climate change and build a more resilient future for ourselves and future generations. Let's act now to address this urgent issue and create a better future for all.

Structure	Language Analysis	Language Features
Title **Date** **Author**	Let's Cool Down and Fight for Change 28 December 2023 B. Nathan	**Title** – tells us what the blog is called. **Date** – the date and year the blog was written. **Author** – the writer.
We introduce the blog by including: Context Date Form Author Title Contention Audience Tone	Climate change and global warming have been in the news all of 2023. We have been reading about and watching videos on extreme weather conditions and the damage they have caused to buildings, human and animal lives, and the environment. In this blog dated 28 December 2023, and titled *Let's Cool Down and Fight for Change*, the author B. Nathan discusses the extreme climate issues we are currently facing. Beginning with an anxious tone, the author contends that most if not all extreme weathers are caused by human manufactured global warming. She goes on to provide facts and figures from various sources to support the contention that if we do not do something about this issue soon, the devastating consequences could be irreversible throughout the world. This blog is directed at all of us, including our governments as global warming and climate change is an issue created by humans but affects all life on the planet.	We type the title of the blog in *italics*. Present tense. The form Context Date Contention Audience Tone Author

Unlocking Genre 188

Body Paragraph 1 As this blog has an image at the beginning, we can analyse this first. We will now begin to use the **TEEL** (Topic sentence, Evidence, Explanation, Linking sentence) strategy.	The blog begins with a picture of a tree divided by two sides of different climates. On one side, we can see the ground covered by green grass and the tree looking healthy. On the other side, we can see the dry and cracked ground and the tree dying. This immediately sets the tone that the author may be worried and disappointed with the current climate conditions. She uses this image to persuade us to think about what can happen to earth due to global warming and extreme weathers right from the beginning of this blog. This is an effective way to create an image in our minds of what could happen if we do not act to combat global warming.	Topic sentence Explain what we can see in the image. Evidence from the blog. Explanation of HOW the reader is persuaded. Tone Linking sentence – links back to the topic sentence.
Body Paragraph 2 In this analysis, we are looking at one paragraph at a time. We will now begin to use the **TEEL** (Topic sentence, Evidence, Explanation, Linking sentence) strategy.	In the first paragraph, the author uses the phrase "most pressing issue" to influence the reader to understand that despite there being many issues in our world today, climate change is on top of the list. The passionate and anxious tones of this start is further supported with a list of events such as "melting ice caps", "rising sea levels", and the recent wild weather hitting some Australian states during Christmas and Boxing Day. She then goes on to give examples of other natural disasters that happened in 2023 around the globe such as the Turkish earthquakes that "killed more than fifty thousand people". Statistics like this gives a clearer picture of the impact of the natural disaster on human life and makes us think about how dangerous the results of global warming could be to life on this planet. Including expert opinion that scientists think these conditions may get worse as the earth gets warmer gives the problem more credibility and highlights the call to action that we need to do something about this as soon as possible.	Topic sentence Evidence from the blog. Explanation of HOW the reader is persuaded. Tone Linking sentence – links back to the topic sentence.
Body Paragraph 3 In this analysis, we are looking at one paragraph at a time. We will now begin to use the **TEEL** (Topic sentence, Evidence, Explanation, Linking sentence) strategy.	In the second paragraph, the author begins with the statistics that 97% of scientists acknowledge that the main reason for the extreme climate changes we are currently experiencing is the emission of "greenhouse gasses." She further asserts that this is due to human beings cutting down forests and "burning fossil fuels" to create energy for our daily needs such as electricity and transportation. These accusations link back to the call to action and allow the reader to understand that it may be possible to reverse the situation by changing some human habits. The author then goes on to quote the UNEP's frightening numbers of how the emission of 59.1 gigatonnes of carbon dioxide in 2019 made it the "second hottest year on record" This gives an immediate link between the amount of emission and the heat produced, therefore bringing it back to how human activity is directly linked to global warming and climate change. The reader is again included in the problem and therefore, its possible solution.	Topic sentence Evidence from the blog. Explanation of HOW the reader is persuaded. Tone Linking sentence – links back to the topic sentence.

Body Paragraph 4 In this analysis, we are looking at one paragraph at a time. We will now begin to use the **TEEL** (Topic sentence, Evidence, Explanation, Linking sentence) strategy.	The third paragraph explores how climate change mostly impacts "marginalised and vulnerable communities" such as indigenous groups and people living in poverty. She supports this argument with the United Nations' data that "30% of the world's population" experience highly dangerous heat waves for more than half a month in a year. This creates empathy and appeals to the readers' sense of justice and responsibility for the many innocent people who are affected by our actions. By doing this, the author is trying to convince the readers that their actions may impact strangers they have never met. This again includes the readers by expressing that all our actions matter to every person living on earth.	Topic sentence Evidence from the blog. Explanation of HOW the reader is persuaded. Tone Linking sentence – links back to the topic sentence.
Body Paragraph 5 In this analysis, we are looking at one paragraph at a time. We will now begin to use the **TEEL** (Topic sentence, Evidence, Explanation, Linking sentence) strategy.	In the fourth paragraph, the author balances the bad news by changing her tone to a more hopeful and optimistic one on what can be done in order to "combat climate change". She adds the recommendation of lowering gas emission by 7.6 % yearly by UNEP and how this can be achieved "through a combination of individual and collective efforts". This inclusive language brings the reader into the loop that they too can make a difference and be a part of the solution. The author then gives a list of possibilities of using natural and renewable sources such as "solar and wind power". She also appeals to the governments to create laws, restoration programmes, and invest money into "clean energy infrastructure." This is an indirect appeal to the readers to choose their governments well. This creates an ethical image of the author and persuades the readers to agree with the author's recommendations that there are many solutions to this problem and we can beat this if we all work together with the support of our governments.	Topic sentence Evidence from the blog. Explanation of HOW the reader is persuaded. Tone Linking sentence – links back to the topic sentence.
Conclusion	The author concludes her blog by giving us hope that the solution to this problem is possible if we all work together. After exploring both the facts of what is currently happening and the possibilities of a positive change, she ends her blog by her inclusive call to action that we need to "address" the problem now so we can all have a "better future."	Topic sentence Signals that we are ending our analysis. Evidence from the blog. Explanation of HOW the reader is persuaded. Tone Linking sentence – links back to the topic sentence.

Discussion questions:

1. Why do you think this blog's language analysis is mostly written in the present tense?
2. What does the title tell us? Do you think it is important to have a title/ Why?
3. How does analysing one paragraph at a time help us?
4. How does using the TEEL strategy help us?
5. What do you already know about blogs and language analysis?
6. Do you know a famous blogger from your home country? Share the main message of their blogs with your friends?
7. Do you enjoy reading blogs in your home language? Why?

Model Text – Non-Annotated

December 28, 2023
By B. Nathan
Let's Cool Down and Fight for Change

Global warming and climate change is one of the most pressing issues facing our planet today. As global temperatures continue to rise, we are seeing an increase in extreme weather events, melting ice caps, and rising sea levels. We recently saw extreme wild weather bringing large hailstones and torrential rains on the states of Victoria, New South Wales, and Queensland on Christmas and Boxing Day, leaving many without electricity and life-threatening property damage. Various other natural disasters around the world were constantly in the news headlines in 2023. These included the massive twin earthquakes in Turkey on 6 February that killed more than fifty thousand people, devastating storms that caused flooding in many parts of the world, volcanic eruptions, bushfires, and many more. Scientists think that these types of extreme weather conditions with become more serious and dangerous as our earth continues to get warmer. It is clear that action must be taken to reduce our impact on the environment and address this urgent issue.

Over 97% of scientists agree that one of the primary causes of climate change is the emission of greenhouse gases, such as carbon dioxide, methane, and nitrous oxide, from human activities like burning fossil fuels, deforestation, and agriculture. Scientists also agree that the rate of carbon emissions is the highest it has been in 66 million years. These gases trap heat in the atmosphere, leading to the greenhouse effect and resulting in the warming of the planet. According to the United Nations Environment Programme (UNEP), total greenhouse emissions in 2019 reached an extreme high of 59.1 gigatonnes of carbon dioxide. It made 2019 the second hottest year on record.

It is also important to recognise that climate change disproportionately affects marginalised communities, such as low-income and Indigenous populations, who often bear the brunt of extreme weather events and environmental degradation. According to the United Nations, 30% of the world's population is exposed to deadly heat waves more than 20 days per year. Addressing climate change must be done in a just and equitable manner, with consideration given to those who are most vulnerable.

To combat climate change, we must act to reduce our greenhouse gas emissions. According to UNEP, we need to explore ways to continuously reduce greenhouse gas emissions by 7.6% every year up to the year 2030. This can be achieved through a combination of individual and collective efforts, including the adoption of renewable energy sources like solar and wind power, energy-efficient buildings, and sustainable transportation. Governments can also play a significant role in reducing emissions through policies to restore natural spaces both on land and in water, investments in clean energy infrastructure, and setting targets and timelines to lower their dependency on energy produced by carbon fuel.

The impact of climate change is already being felt around the world, but it is not too late to act. By reducing our greenhouse gas emissions and transitioning to a more sustainable way of life, we can help reduce the worst effects of climate change and build a more resilient future for ourselves and future generations. Let's act now to address this urgent issue and create a better future for all.

Blog Language Analysis
Title of blog: *Let's Cool Down and Fight the Change*
Date: 28 December 2023
Author: B. Nathan

Climate change and global warming have been in the news all of 2023. We have been reading about and watching videos on extreme weather conditions and the damage they have caused to buildings, human and animal lives, and the environment. In this blog dated 28 December 2023, and titled *Let's Cool Down and Fight for Change*, the author Boney Nathan discusses the extreme climate issues we are currently facing. Beginning with an anxious tone, the author contends that most if not all extreme weathers are caused by human manufactured global warming. She goes on to provide facts and figures from various sources to support the contention that if we do not do something about this issue soon, the devastating consequences could be irreversible throughout the world. This blog is directed at all of us, including our governments as global warming and climate change is an issue created by humans but affects all life on the planet.

The blog begins with a picture of a tree divided by two sides of different climates. On one side, we can see the ground covered by green grass and the tree looking healthy. On the other side, we can see the dry and cracked ground and the tree dying. This immediately sets the tone that the author may be worried and disappointed with the current climate conditions. She uses this image to persuade us to think about what can happen to earth due to global warming and extreme weathers right from the beginning of this blog. This is an effective way to create an image in our minds of what could happen if we do not act to combat global warming.

In the first paragraph, the author uses the phrase "most pressing issue" to influence the reader to understand that despite there being many issues in our world today, climate change is on top of the list. The passionate and anxious tones of this start is further supported with a list of events such as "melting ice caps", "rising sea levels", and the recent wild weather hitting some Australian states during Christmas and Boxing Day. She then goes on to give examples of other natural disasters that happened in 2023 around the globe such as the Turkish earthquakes that "killed more than fifty thousand people". Statistics like this gives a clearer picture of the impact of the natural disaster on human life and makes us think about how dangerous the results of global warming could be to life on this planet. Including expert opinion that scientists think these conditions may get worse as the earth gets warmer gives the problem more credibility and highlights the call to action that we need to do something about this as soon as possible.

In the second paragraph, the author begins with the statistics that 97% of scientists acknowledge that the main reason for the extreme climate changes we are currently experiencing is the emission of "greenhouse gasses." She further asserts that this is due to human beings cutting down forests and "burning fossil fuels" to create energy for our daily needs such as electricity and transportation. These accusations link back to the call to action and allow the reader to understand that it may be possible to reverse the situation by changing some human habits. The author then goes on to quote the UNEP's frightening numbers of how the emission of 59.1 gigatonnes of carbon dioxide in 2019 made it the "second hottest year on record" This gives an immediate link between the amount of emission and the heat produced, therefore bringing it back to how human activity is directly linked to global warming and climate change. The reader is again included in the problem and therefore, its possible solution.

The third paragraph explores how climate change mostly impacts "marginalised and vulnerable communities" such as indigenous groups and people living in poverty. She supports this argument with the United Nations' data that "30% of the world's population" experience highly dangerous heat waves for more than half a month in a year. This creates empathy and appeals to the readers' sense of justice and responsibility for the many innocent people who are affected by our actions. By doing this, the author is trying to convince the readers that their actions may impact strangers they have never met. This again includes the readers by expressing that all our actions matter to every person living on earth.

In the fourth paragraph, the author balances the bad news by changing her tone to a more hopeful and optimistic one on what can be done in order to "combat climate change". She adds the recommendation of lowering gas emission by 7.6 % yearly by UNEP and how this can be achieved "through a combination of individual and collective efforts". This inclusive language brings the reader into the loop that they too can make a difference and be a part of the solution. The author then gives a list of possibilities of using natural and renewable sources such as "solar and wind power". She also appeals to the governments to create laws, restoration programmes, and invest money into "clean energy infrastructure." This is an indirect appeal to the readers to choose their governments well. This creates an ethical image of the author and persuades the readers to agree with the author's recommendations that there are many solutions to this problem and we can beat this if we all work together with the support of our governments.

The author concludes her blog by giving us hope that the solution to this problem is possible if we all work together. After exploring both the facts of what is currently happening and the possibilities of a positive change, she ends her blog by her inclusive call to action that we need to "address" the problem now so we can all have a "better future."

Reading and Viewing Activities
A: Word Level

1. List all the verbs you can see.

2. The verbs are written in the _____ tenses because _____.
3. What are the different meanings of the phrases 'climate change' and 'global warming'?
4. Why do you think we use special words to write a language analysis?
5. List THREE words or phrases that tell you that this is a language analysis. Give a reason why you think so. One example has been done for you.

Word/phrase from the passage	My reason
"Beginning with an anxious tone, the author contends that…"	This tells me that we are analysing how the language used by the author shows what they are feeling.

6. Why do you think we use " " (quotation marks) when we use words or phrases as evidence from the blog?

7. List TWO new words you learnt from each paragraph of the Language Analysis of the blog. What do they mean? Write your own sentences using the new words.

Sub-heading	New words	Meaning	Write your own sentence using the word.
Paragraph 1			
Paragraph 2			
Paragraph 3			
Paragraph 4			
Paragraph 5			
Paragraph 6			
Paragraph 7			

8. What did you do to find the meaning of new words?
   _____

9. Give an example from the language analysis for each device below. Explain how it helps the audience.

Language analysis device	Example	How does it help the audience?
context		
form		
audience		
contention		
tone		
author		

B: Sentence Level

Answer the questions using complete sentences.

1. Why do you think we need to acknowledge the author of the blog?
   _____

2. Why do we need to include context in our language analysis introduction?
   _____

3. What is this language analysis about?
   _____

4. Why do you think we analyse different aspects of the blog?
   _____

5. Look at the "HOW this influences the readers?" part of each paragraph:
   a. Why do you think we need to analyse this aspect?
      _____
   b. How does this give credibility to our analysis? How do you know this?
      _____

6. List three sentences from the introduction section that give us important information about this blog.
   a. _____
   b. _____
   c. _____

7. Answer the questions below:

What do we do in the conclusion of a language analysis?	
Does the analysis help the reader understand the blog better? Why?	

8. List THREE interesting ideas about this blog from the analysis. One example has been done for you.

The introduction gives us some context about the blog.

Write your own beginning sentence for each these sub-headings.

Sub-heading	Sentence from the analysis	My own sentence
Introduction	Climate change and global warming have been in the news all of 2023.	
Conclusion	The author concludes her blog by giving us hope that the solution to this problem is possible if we all work together.	

C: Text Level

Write ONE sentence to explain what each paragraph of the blog is about. Then write ONE sentence to explain what the language analysis is about. Answer the two questions that follow.

	The Blog	The Language Analysis
Paragraph 1		
Paragraph 2		
Paragraph 3		
Paragraph 4		
Paragraph 5		
Paragraph 6		
Paragraph 7		
Think about how the language analysis of the blog is different from the blog itself. a. How is the language analysis different to the blog? b. How will you use this idea in your own analysis?	a. b.	

Functional Grammar

	Describe	What?	Extra Information
Some	scary	videos	on YouTube.
		weather	
		environment	
		image	
		earthquakes	
		gasses	
		blog	

D: Writing

Choose a whole class blog (Teacher's choice). Write your own Language Analysis about it. Use the sub-headings to help you plan.

Title of blog: Date: Author:	
Introduction We type the title of the blog in *italics*. Present tense. The form Context Date Contention Audience Tone Author	
Body Paragraph 1 TEEL	
Body Paragraph 2 TEEL	
Body Paragraph 3 TEEL	
Conclusion	

Part Four – Advanced/Consolidating Level – Language Analysis
Genre 3, Text 2
Teacher's Notes: What is a Language Analysis?

Language analysis is the study of how language is used to convey meaning and influence or persuade readers. It involves analysing written or spoken language to identify syntax and semantics, literary techniques, and linguistic strategies that a writer or speaker uses to communicate a particular message or idea.

Language analysis can take many forms, such as literary analysis, discourse analysis, and rhetorical analysis. It can involve analysing the use of language in a single text or across a range of texts or genres. It is commonly used in fields such as literature, media studies, linguistics, and communication studies, as well as in business, politics, and other areas where effective communication is important.

When analysing language, it is important to consider the context in which it is used, including the audience, the purpose of the text, and the cultural and social factors that may influence its interpretation. Common techniques used in language analysis include identifying the use of figurative language, rhetorical devices, and persuasive appeals such as logos (logic), ethos (credibility), and pathos (emotional connection).

For English as an Additional Language/Dialect (EAL/D) students, language analysis is an important skill that can help them develop critical thinking and analytical skills, as well as improve their ability to deconstruct the nuances of the English language more effectively. They may come across the opportunity to do this through their every day connection with social media, news, advertisements, global issues, current trends, etc.

Features of a Language Analysis – Letter to Editor

- Introduction – provides background information about the letter (title, author, language), its genre, overall message, and its context.
- Summary – a brief summary of the text highlighting:
    - form
    - context
    - date
    - contention
    - tone etc.
- Analysis of how the examples below are used to persuade the audience:
    - Content – the author's use of themes, symbols, motifs, etc.
    - Theme – author's message
    - Literary Techniques/Devices – dialogue, figurative language, imagery, etc.
    - Author's Voice – sentence structure, grammar, humour, etc.
    - Conflict – real, perceived, projected, etc.
    - Data – author's use of graphs, numbers, etc.
- Evidence to support the analysis – specific examples, quotes, etc.
- Conclusion – main findings, what that means, personal opinion, etc.
- Accurate – based on the language being analysed.
- Clearly and logically organised – may include heading, sub-headings, conclusion etc.
- Objective and subjective language – facts and personal opinions.
- Language features – metalanguage, technical terms, etc.

Text 2 – Language Analysis
Letter to Editor

Writing a language analysis about a letter to an editor allows students to critically examine and evaluate a text by deconstructing its content, structure, and language features. Analysing a letter can help EAL/D students explore and discuss literary devices that exist in the English language. This will create awareness of the nuances of the language and encourage them to take risks in their daily writing tasks. Writing simple language analysis at the advanced level allows students to go deeper into experimenting with the fundamental skills for analytical writing.

Part Four, Genre 3 – Language Analysis
Letter to Editor

Word Bank

dispute	not agreeing
blaming	saying it is another person's fault
anecdotal	just listening to what people are saying without finding out if it was true.
factual data	facts with numbers and graphs
infuriating	making someone very angry
backlash	saying or doing something against someone
numerous	many
disregard	not caring
anxious	worried
equity	being fair to everyone
discrimination	being unfair to someone because of their age, race, skin colour etc.
financial	using money
crucial	very important
genuinely	truly
applauded	being praised or cheered

Model Text – Annotated for whole class discussion

Letter to Editor
B Nathan
21 Poster St
Mosley
VICTORIA 3331

To
The Editor
The Victorian News
57 Dower Rd
Breland
VICTORIA 3232
27 December 2023

Dear Editor,

I am writing to dispute your recent series of articles titled 'The MENTALITY of Youth' (June to December 2023) where you have published interviews and letters from the public, blaming and shaming young people for many of the social problems and issues currently taking place in our society. Interestingly, many of these are based on anecdotal experiences and are not backed up by any factual data.

One of the issues, I found most infuriating was the backlash against young people taking to the streets to protest against numerous national and international matters such as "the Voice", climate change, the war in Gaza, to name a few. According to some of your 'well-informed' public, young people should focus on finishing their education and leave these matters to the politicians and adult members of the society. I would like to highlight the fact that leaving these matters to those in charge is exactly what has brought us wars, a dying earth, and total disregard for the well-being of Indigenous people.

According to Mission Australia, 44% of young people are anxious about the environment, 31% think that there are ongoing issues with equity and discrimination, another 31% worry about financial difficulties including homelessness, and 30% consider mental health as a crucial issue. As a young person, I can assure you that my generation has lost its trust in governments and other public figures to solve our problems. Most of us feel that there is no point in completing our education if there is not going to be a peaceful and healthy world to live in.

We genuinely feel that it is time for us to be seen and heard. Public protests are within our legal rights and having the courage to stand up and demonstrate our concerns in a peaceful and safe manner should in fact be encouraged and applauded. History has shown that many positive changes in the world were brought on by young people taking to the streets, the very young people who may now be criticising us for doing exactly what their generation did. It would be a welcome change if those who are against our actions actually had robust conversations with us so we can create a better understanding for both sides. Would it be possible for your newspaper to create such an opportunity through the same series?

Thank you.
B Nathan

Structure	Language Analysis	Language Features
Title **Date** **Author**	Letter to Editor 29 December 2023 B Nathan	**Title** – tells us what we are analysing. **Date** – the date and year the letter was written. **Author** – the writer
We introduce the letter by including: Context Date Form Author Title Contention Audience Tone	B Nathan, a young person has written a letter to the editor of *The Victorian News* on 27 December 2023, to highlight an issue he has with a series of articles titled 'The MENTALITY of Youth' published between June and December of 2023. He is offended that the newspaper has allowed the public to "blame and shame" youth for current social issues, especially public protests, without any facts to back up the accusations. Although this letter is addressed to the editor, B Nathan is aiming its content to the government, politicians, and the older generation that contributed to the series of articles.	We type the name of the publication in *italics*. The form Context Date Contention Audience Tone Author
Body Paragraph 1 In this analysis, we are looking at one paragraph at a time. We will now begin to use the **TEEL** (Topic sentence, Evidence, Explanation, Linking sentence) strategy.	In the opening paragraph, the writer begins with his contention against a series of articles that the newspaper has published for the past six months. He begins his letter with the word "dispute" making it very clear that he is unhappy and does not agree with what the newspaper has published. He further contends that the newspaper has allowed the public to accuse young people as the source of "current social problems" without any evidence, immediately getting younger readers on his side by contesting the authenticity of the claims made in the series of articles.	Topic sentence Evidence from the letter. Explanation of HOW the reader is persuaded. Tone Linking sentence – links back to the topic sentence.
Body Paragraph 2 In this analysis, we are looking at one paragraph at a time. We will now begin to use the **TEEL** (Topic sentence, Evidence, Explanation, Linking sentence) strategy.	In the second paragraph, he focuses on the main issue that has extremely annoyed him. He lists a few current issues that are popular with young people, further gaining support from his age group. He uses sarcasm when he puts the phrase "well informed public" in inverted commas, further discrediting the claims they have made. Asserting that allowing people "in charge" to solve these problems has actually led to "wars", environmental and Indigenous people's issues, he directs his contention to the people in power while capturing the hearts of the youth he is standing up for.	Topic sentence Evidence from the letter. Explanation of HOW the reader is persuaded. Tone Linking sentence – links back to the topic sentence.

Body Paragraph 3 In this analysis, we are looking at one paragraph at a time. We will now begin to use the **TEEL** (Topic sentence, Evidence, Explanation, Linking sentence) strategy.	In the third paragraph of his letter, he continues to destroy the public opinion published in the newspaper by supporting his argument with data from Mission Australia to highlight that the youth of today do care about important issues. Using the phrase "my generation" further isolates the governments, politicians and the general public while banding together the young people of his generation as one important group. The data he provides further strengthens his argument that young people want authentic solutions to their problems, once again including the people of his generation in his letter.	Topic sentence Evidence from the letter. Explanation of HOW the reader is persuaded. Tone Linking sentence links back to the topic sentence.
Body Paragraph 4 In this analysis, we are looking at one paragraph at a time. We will now begin to use the **TEEL** (Topic sentence, Evidence, Explanation, Linking sentence) strategy.	In his final paragraph, the writer uses "we" to involve all young people in what he considers is within their "legal rights" to fight for a better world, as history has shown. He links this back to his contention that the very public who have accused his generation for current social issues, were the same people who took action during their youth. This is a clever way to get the group of people he is writing against to start agreeing with him. At the end of his letter, he offers a peaceful solution to advocate change and understanding through dialogue between the different generations, further pulling in readers of all ages to support his arguments.	Topic sentence Evidence from the letter. Explanation of HOW the reader is persuaded. Tone Linking sentence – links back to the topic sentence.
Conclusion	In conclusion, this letter to the editor tackles the issues the writer has with the series of articles published The Victorian News while offering valid counter arguments and a possible solution to his contention. The writer has used effective evidence and inclusive language such as "create a better understanding" to get the readers to agree with his arguments. He ends his letter with an emotional flashback to the past of the people who have accused young people of creating social unrest, therefore getting them to remember their own youth and the ideal they fought for.	Topic sentence Signals that we are ending our analysis. Evidence from the letter. Explanation of HOW the reader is persuaded. Tone Linking sentence – links back to the topic sentence.

Discussion questions:

1. Why do you think this letter to editor language analysis is mostly written in the present tense?
2. What does the title tell us? Do you think it is important to have a title/ Why?
3. How does analysing one paragraph at a time help us?
4. How does using the TEEL strategy help us?
5. What do you already know about letters to editors and language analysis?
6. Do you know a famous writer from your home country? Share the main message of their work with your friends?
7. Do you enjoy reading letters to editors in your home language? Why?

Model Text – Non-Annotated

Letter to Editor
B Nathan
21 Poster St
Mosley
VICTORIA 3331

To
The Editor
The Victorian News
57 Dower Rd
Breland
VICTORIA 3232
29 December 2023

Dear Editor,

I am writing to dispute your recent series of articles titled 'The MENTALITY of Youth' (June to December 2023) where you have published interviews and letters from the public, blaming and shaming young people for many of the social problems and issues currently taking place in our society. Interestingly, many of these are based on anecdotal experiences and are not backed up by any factual data.

One of the issues, I found most infuriating was the backlash against young people taking to the streets to protest against numerous national and international matters such as "the Voice", climate change, the war in Gaza, to name a few. According to some of your 'well-informed' public, young people should focus on finishing their education and leave these matters to the politicians and adult members of the society. I would like to highlight the fact that leaving these matters to those in charge is exactly what has brought us wars, a dying earth, and total disregard for the well-being of Indigenous people.

According to Mission Australia, 44% of young people are anxious about the environment, 31% think that there are ongoing issues with equity and discrimination, another 31% worry about financial difficulties including homelessness, and 30% consider mental health as a crucial issue. As a young person, I can assure you that my generation has lost its trust in governments and other public figures to solve our problems. Most of us feel that there is no point in completing our education if there is not going to be a peaceful and healthy world to live in.

We genuinely feel that it is time for us to be seen and heard. Public protests are within our legal rights and having the courage to stand up and demonstrate our concerns in a peaceful and safe manner should in fact be encouraged and applauded. History has shown that many positive changes in the world were brought on by young people taking to the streets, the very young people who may now be criticising us for doing exactly what their generation did. It would be a welcome change if those who are against our actions actually had robust conversations with us so we can create a better understanding for both sides. Would it be possible for your newspaper to create such an opportunity through the same series?
Thank you.
B Nathan

Letter to Editor Language Analysis
Date: 29 December 2023
Author: B Nathan

B Nathan, a young person has written a letter to the editor of The Victorian News on 29 December 2023, to highlight an issue he has with a series of articles titled 'The MENTALITY of Youth' published between June and December of 2023. He is offended that the newspaper has allowed the public to "blame and shame" youth for current social issues, especially public protests, without any facts to back up the accusations. Although this letter is addressed to the editor, B Nathan is aiming its content to the government, politicians, and the older generation that contributed to the series of articles.

In the opening paragraph, the writer begins with his contention against a series of articles that the newspaper has published for the past six months. He begins his letter with the word "dispute" making it very clear that he is unhappy and does not agree with what the newspaper has published. He further contends that the newspaper has allowed the public to accuse young people as the source of "current social problems" without any evidence, immediately getting younger readers on his side by contesting the authenticity of the claims made in the series of articles.

In the second paragraph, he focuses on the main issue that has extremely annoyed him. He lists a few current issues that are popular with young people, further gaining support from his age group. He uses sarcasm when he puts the phrase "well informed public" in inverted commas, further discrediting the claims they have made. Asserting that allowing people "in charge" to solve these problems has actually led to "wars", environmental and Indigenous people's issues, he directs his contention to the people in power while capturing the hearts of the youth he is standing up for.

In the third paragraph of his letter, he continues to destroy the public opinion published in the newspaper by supporting his argument with data from Mission Australia to highlight that the youth of today do care about important issues. Using the phrase "my generation" further isolates the governments, politicians and the general public while banding together the young people of his generation as one important group. The data he provides further strengthens his argument that young people want authentic solutions to their problems, once again including the people of his generation in his letter.

In his final paragraph, the writer uses "we" to involve all young people in what he considers is within their "legal rights" to fight for a better world, as history has shown. He links this back to his contention that the very public who have accused his generation for current social issues, were the same people who took action during their youth. This is a clever way to get the group of people he is writing against to start agreeing with him. At the end of his letter, he offers a peaceful solution to advocate change and understanding through dialogue between the different generations, further pulling in readers of all ages to support his arguments.

In conclusion, this letter to the editor tackles the issues the writer has with the series of articles published The Victorian News while offering valid counter arguments and a possible solution to his contention. The writer has used effective evidence and inclusive language such as "create a better understanding" to get the readers to agree with his arguments. He ends his letter with an emotional flashback to the past of the people who have accused young people of creating social unrest, therefore getting them to remember their own youth and the ideal they fought for.

Reading and Viewing Activities

A: Word Level

1. List all the verbs you can see.

   [ ]

2. The verbs are written in the _____ tenses because _____.
3. List THREE words that tell you this is a letter:

4. Why do you think we use special words to write a language analysis?
5. List THREE words or phrases that tell you that this is a language analysis. Give a reason why you think so. One example has been done for you.

Word/phrase from the passage	My reason
"B Nathan, a young person has written a letter to the editor…"	This tells me that we are analysing a letter written to an editor.

6. Why do you think we use " " (quotation marks) when we use words or phrases as evidence from the blog?

7. List TWO new words you learnt from each paragraph of the Language Analysis of the letter to the editor. What do they mean? Write your own sentences using the new words.

Sub-heading	New words	Meaning	Write your own sentence using the word.
Paragraph 1			
Paragraph 2			
Paragraph 3			
Paragraph 4			
Paragraph 5			
Paragraph 6			

8. What did you do to find the meaning of new words?

9. Give an example from the language analysis for each device below. Explain how it helps the audience.

Language analysis device	Example	How does it help the audience?
context		
form		
audience		
contention		
tone		
author		

B: Sentence Level

Answer the questions using complete sentences.

1. Why do you think we need to acknowledge the author of the letter?
   _____
2. Why do we need to include context in our language analysis introduction?
   _____
3. What is this language analysis about?
   _____
4. Why do you think we analyse different aspects of the letter?
   _____
5. Look at the "HOW this influences the readers?" part of each paragraph:
   a. Why do you think we need to analyse this aspect?
      _____
   b. How does this give credibility to our analysis? How do you know this?
      _____
6. List three sentences from the introduction section that give us important information about this letter.
   a. _____
   b. _____
   c. _____

7. Answer the questions below:

What do we do in the conclusion of a language analysis?	
Does the analysis help the reader understand the letter better? Why?	

8. List THREE interesting ideas about this letter from the analysis. One example has been done for you.

The introduction gives us some context about the letter.

Write your own beginning sentence for each these paragraphs.

Paragraph	Sentence from the analysis	My own sentence
Paragraph 1	B Nathan, a young person has written a letter to the editor of The Victorian News on 29 December 2023, to highlight an issue he has with a series of articles titled 'The MENTALITY of Youth' published between June and December of 2023.	
Paragraph 5	In conclusion, this letter to the editor tackles the issues the writer has with the series of articles published The Victorian News while offering valid counter arguments and a possible solution to his contention.	

Unlocking Genre   207

C: Text Level

Write ONE sentence to explain what each paragraph of the letter is about. Then write ONE sentence to explain what the language analysis is about. Answer the two questions that follow.

	The Letter	The Language Analysis
Paragraph 1		
Paragraph 2		
Paragraph 3		
Paragraph 4		
Paragraph 5		
Think about how the language analysis of the letter is different from the letter itself. a. How is the language analysis different to the letter? b. How will you use this idea in your own analysis?	a. b.	

Functional Grammar

	Describe	What?	Extra Information
A	young	person	wrote a letter.
		newspaper	
		letter	
		readers	
		opinion	
		solution	
		editor	

D: Writing

Choose a whole class letter to an editor (Teacher's choice). Write your own Language Analysis about it. Use the sub-headings to help you plan.

Title: Date: Author:	
Introduction We type the title of the newspaper in *italics*. Present tense. The form Context Date Contention Audience Tone Author	
Body Paragraph 1 TEEL	
Body Paragraph 2 TEEL	
Body Paragraph 3 TEEL	
Conclusion	

References

Ahn Do & Suzanne Do (2011) *The Little Refugee*. Retrieved from: https://fliphtml5.com/ljetg/cjle/basic (Accessed: 31 August 2023).

BBC. (2023) *Bitesize*. Available at: https://www.bbc.co.uk/bitesize/topics/zg87xnb (Accessed: 21 July 2023).

Britannica Kids (2023) *Solar System*. Available at: https://kids.britannica.com/kids/article/solar-system/353789 (Accesses: 4 August 2023).

Byju's (2023) *Human Respiratory System*. Available at: https://byjus.com/biology/human-respiratory-system/ (Accessed: 11 August 2023).

Ducksters. (2022) *Ancient Egypt for Kids*. Available at: https://www.ducksters.com/history/ancient_egypt.php (Accessed: 21 July 2023).

J. Marsden & S. Tan (1998). *The Rabbits*. Retrieved from: chrome-extension://efaidnbmnnnibpcajpcglclefindmkaj/https://st-marys.hackney.sch.uk/wp-content/uploads/2021/01/The-Rabbits-story-PDF.pdf (Accessed: 8 September 2023).

KidCyber. (2022) *First Fleet*. Available at: https://www.kidcyber.com.au/first-fleet (Accessed: 25 July 2023).

Kiddle. (2023) *First Fleet facts for kids*. Available at: https://kids.kiddle.co/First_Fleet (Accessed: 25 July 2023).

Nemours KidsHealth (2023) *Your Lungs & Respiratory System*. Available at: https://kidshealth.org/en/kids/lungs.html (Accessed: 11 August 2023).

Sciencing (2023) *The Characteristics of the Eight Planets*. Available at: https://sciencing.com/characteristics-eight-planets-8332488.html (Accessed: 4 August 2023).

The Road Not Taken (1915) *Public Domain Poetry*. Available at https://www.public-domain-poetry.com/robert-lee-frost/road-not-taken-1222 (Accessed: 29 November 2023).

The Planets (2010-2023) *Planet Facts*. Available at: https://theplanets.org/planets/ (Accessed: 4 August 2023).

The Ultimate Film Techniques List (2022). *Matrix Education*. Available at https://www.matrix.edu.au/essential-guide-english-techniques/ultimate-film-techniques-list/ (Accessed: 6 December 2023).

Twinkl (2023) *What is the Respiratory System?* Available at: https://www.twinkl.com.au/teaching-wiki/respiratory-system (Accessed: 11 August 2023).

www.ingramcontent.com/pod-product-compliance
Lightning Source LLC
Chambersburg PA
CBHW081917090526
44590CB00019B/3386